The
Mathematics
Of
Retirement

Praise For
The Mathematics Of Retirement

"Rooted in integrity, life experience, and a genuine respect for personal purpose, this book brings both clarity and heart to retirement planning. Shaped by a life lived across cultures, Reid offers thoughtful guidance, reminding readers that financial decisions are ultimately about people, purpose and the stories that shape us."
—**Lt Col Dan Rooney**, Founder of Folds of Honor, Speaker, and Author of *Fly Into The Wind* and *A Patriots Calling*

"Having known Reid since 2011, I have come to value his commitment to his more than 2,000 clients and community. The son of immigrants, he is The American Dream. I have watched him build a company with more than 20 team members serving families in California and Arizona.

And, he has helped these retirees while balancing a strong home life. The father of three, two of his and Smyrna's children have interned here at Advisors Excel. Safeguard is becoming a generational retirement planning firm.

Being a numbers nerd myself, I was drawn to this book. *The Mathematics Of Retirement* uses Reid's love of chess as a metaphor for utilizing measured and logical moves to develop retirement plans. Like Reid, this book is worth your time and attention."
—**David Callanan**, Co-Founder of Advisors Excel

"At its heart, this book is about the power of personal stories and how Reid's disciplined planning approach offers the best opportunity for a long and secure retirement.

As a chess player, Reid is a planner by nature. Nothing is left to chance.

Thoughtful is the word I most associate with my colleague of more than a decade.

Want to find out about a person's true character and attitudes? Spend personal time with them. Our two families have travelled together for years. When no one is around, I have found Reid to be just as committed to his thousands of clients as he is when visiting with them in the Safeguard offices.

I am excited about this book. It has been a long time coming and is very readable. Enjoy."

—**Cody Foster**, Co-Founder of Advisors Excel

"*The Mathematics Of Retirement* approaches retirement planning with the mindset of thinking several moves ahead, framing retirement as a long-term process rather than a single decision. From the opening moves of wealth building to the endgame of financial preservation, this book presents retirement as a series of intentional choices made over time.

It emphasizes that retirement is not just about money, but about sustaining a lifestyle, protecting a legacy, and planning with a gambit from the earliest stages of life through career checkmate. What you hold is more than a guide; it's a clear, thoughtful companion for building a secure, meaningful, and well-lived retirement."

—**Robert A. Boyd, II**, COO of Tyler Perry Studios

The Mathematics *Of* Retirement

How To Safeguard Your Future

REID ABEDEEN

The Mathematics Of Retirement
How To Safeguard Your Future

No part of this publication may be reproduced or distributed in any form or by any means, without the prior permission of the publisher. Requests for permission should be directed to permissions@indiebooksintl.com, or mailed to Permissions, Indie Books International, 2511 Woodlands Way, Oceanside, CA 92054.

The views and opinions in this book are those of the author at the time of writing this book, and do not reflect the opinions of Indie Books International or its editors.

Neither the publisher nor the author is engaged in rendering legal or other professional services through this book. If expert assistance is required, the services of appropriate professionals should be sought. The publisher and the author shall have neither liability nor responsibility to any person or entity with respect to any loss or damage caused directly or indirectly by the information in this publication.

This content is provided for informational purposes only and is not intended to serve as the basis for financial decisions. All investments are subject to risk including the potential loss of principal. No investment strategy can guarantee a profit or protect against loss in periods of declining values. The information and opinions contained herein that have been obtained from third-party sources are believed to be reliable. Accuracy and completeness cannot be guaranteed.

The Safeguard Planning Playbook™ is a pending trademark of Reid Abedeen.
CFP® and Certified Financial Planner® are registered trademarks of Certified Financial Planner Board of Standards Center for Financial Planning, Inc.
Google® is a registered trademark of Google, LLC.
Morningstar® is a registered trademark of Morningstar, Inc.
Apple ® is a registered trademark of Apple, Inc.
IBM® and Deep Blue® are registered trademarks of International Business Machine Corporation.
Netflix® is a registered trademark of Netflix, Inc.
TikTok® is a registered trademark of TikTok, Ltd.

ISBN-13: 978-1-966168-54-6
Library of Congress Control Number: 2026905854

Designed by Melissa Farr, Back Porch Creative, LLC

Wealth Authority Books
2511 WOODLANDS WAY
OCEANSIDE, CA 92054
www.indiebooksintl.com

Wealth Authority Books is an imprint of Indie Books International®, Inc.

Without the element of enjoyment,
it is not worth trying to excel at anything.
Chess Grandmaster Magnus Carlsen

Dedication

To my parents, Dr. Mustafa Abedeen and Dr. Hikmat Alshaibi,
whose sacrifices and commitment to education taught me
to think boldly, plan wisely, and care deeply.
Everything I do—including this book—began with you.

Contents

Are You Making Bad Retirement Gambits?

I love the game of chess. The game is full of real-life applications. A game of chess often begins with a gambit, a move designed to gain an advantage. The word "gambit" comes from an Italian expression, *dare il gambetto* (to put a leg forward in order to trip someone).[1] A gambit is meant to throw your opponent off their game from the start. That's the goal: to start out strong, even sacrificing a piece, for an advantage later on in the game. But gambits can be risky, and sometimes you are tripping up nobody but yourself.

Opening gambits—perhaps the first ten moves in a chess game—are the subject of countless books. You might do an Indian opening, which is a very defensive play. Or you might do the London opening, which creates many possibilities for subsequent moves. You might do a Queen's gambit where you're taking a big risk, but the payoff could be enormous.

The same is true for your financial plan.

When you are playing chess, there's an opponent, and the opponent sees the moves you make, and does things to disrupt your plan, counter it, and take advantage. That's why you just can't set up a gambit and forget it. I use the chess analogy for this reason. It's an interactive sport. It's a mental game, and you must stay in the game mentally to win.

With that in mind, here are ten bad gambits I see retirees consistently making, and most do not know if the odds are in their favor. Where do you stand on these ten gambits:

1. *Are you taking too much risk?* Risk isn't one-size-fits-all. What's appropriate depends on your stage of life and your personal tolerance for market swings. As you shift from accumulating assets to drawing income, your approach should evolve to reflect your needs and protect what you've built.

2. *Are you employing a strategy contingent on being in a lower tax bracket in retirement?* Taxes are our largest expense every single year. And in the future, they are likely to go up, not down.

3. *Are you paying too much in fees?* Rarely do the people we talk to at our company, Safeguard Investment Advisory Group, have an accurate sense of how much they pay in fees. They don't always show up on their statements. It is a bad bet to just trust and not verify.

4. *Are you skipping a Roth conversion?* No matter what stage of life you are in, you should be considering converting. If you are wagering that your tax bracket will be lower in retirement, you might be losing that bet. Maybe it is time to

bet on higher taxes by moving that 401(k) and IRA money into a Roth account. You can pay the tax man a little now, or you can pay the tax man a lot down the road.

5. *Are you working a plan closely tied to the stock market?* Minimize the impacts of eventual stock market dives. Don't bet your income plan on stocks or even index mutual funds. Remember when the market dropped 30 percent in March of 2020 and 50 percent in the Great Recession of 2007–2009?

6. *Are you ignoring a long-term care plan?* Betting you won't need long-term care could jeopardize your plans if you or your spouse becomes sick.

7. *Are you hoping loved ones are accounted for?* Make sure your assets will be properly transferred to loved ones if you do not spend them all.

8. *Are scammers and identity thieves eyeing you as a target?* The answer is always "yes."

9. *Are you using a cookie-cutter financial plan?* Many feel a typical plan will suit their needs, and there is no need to invest time or resources in a customized plan. One-size-fits-all may work for sweatshirts and bathrobes, but not for retirement plans.

10. *Are you ignoring financial future trends?* Ignoring future trends may be one of the most expensive gambits of all. Economic cycles, tax policy, inflation, longevity, and technology are constantly evolving, and these shifts directly impact retirees. Staying informed—and adjusting your

plan as conditions change—helps ensure your financial strategy isn't built for yesterday's world.

If you are not addressing these ten gambits, chances are your retirement planning is going to be incomplete.

Of course, if you don't make any moves, you are not in the game. So, how do you start strong and play the game well to win the chess game of retirement?

Your Best Moves For Retirement

When I was growing up, my father used to always win when he played me at chess. Don't feel sorry for me; those are the fondest memories of my life. We first started playing chess when I was five years old. Not to say I was competitive, but I wanted to beat him every time.

This book covers what we call *The Safeguard Planning Playbook*™.

The first move is to manage your level of risk. Risk is an important part of the game, and you need to understand it.

Move number two: Are you factoring in taxation? The biggest expense you will have in retirement will likely be taxes. So you need a game plan for Uncle Sam.

Move number three: How much are you paying in fees? The dirty little secret of the financial industry is hidden fees. The financial industry is marvelous at hiding and disguising fees.

Move number four: Are you considering Roth conversions? There is a miracle opportunity in the tax code, and it is not the 401(k) or the IRA; it is the Roth, and you need to understand how to use it in your game plan.

Move number five: Make sure to have income streams separate from the market. The stock market can be a roller coaster ride, and that is no fun. You want a retirement income that is not dependent on the ups and downs of the market.

Move number six: Do you have a long-term care plan? It's sad to say that many of us are going to need long-term care during our retirement years, and many people have just accepted that long-term care insurance is too expensive or is not available. There are solutions to this dilemma.

Move number seven: Are your loved ones accounted for? Mistakes can easily be made when it comes to designating beneficiaries or arranging affairs when you pass on.

Move number eight: Have you protected yourself from scammers and identity thieves? It's one thing to make money, it's another thing to accumulate the money, and it's another thing altogether to keep the money. There are bad people out there who are clever and sophisticated, and they want to steal your money. You need to protect yourself. If I can make an analogy, the bank has security for a reason. They don't leave the safes open. The same should be true about your protection from identity theft.

Move number nine: Financial plans are not "set it and forget it." We live in a volatile world. There's uncertainty. There is change, and there are new discoveries and great innovations. All of this requires you to adjust your game plan as you play the retirement game of chess.

Move number ten: Monitor the financial future trends. Again, you need to educate yourself. You need to be a student of the game. You need to know where the economy, politics, and science are headed so that you can adjust to play to win.

Advisor As Advocate

What is the role of a financial advisor? Is it to sell you a product transactionally? You can walk into any bank, brokerage, or insurance agency for a variety of financial products, and you may or may not get advice along with opening that account or purchasing that financial product.

In this book, I use what I have learned from chess as a metaphor for making the right moves and decisions for retirement. For a moment, indulge me in another sports metaphor. I have a love-hate relationship with golf. I love the game, but I am terrible at it. Recently, I went to the Farmers Insurance Open at Torrey Pines with my wife and kids. Watching the pros in person was a real treat, but what I really paid attention to were the caddies.

One thing I noticed was the communication between the caddy and the professional golfer. Think for a moment about these pro golfers: They can hit the ball better than any caddy, they have strengthened their game over a lifetime to get to this elite level, and they rigorously study every course they play. Why do they need a caddy other than to hold the bag, clean the clubs, and make sure the pro stays hydrated?

Based on what I witnessed, the caddy plays a crucial advisory role. I listened to caddies suggesting where to hit the ball, making note of danger areas ahead and how to avoid them. They paid attention to wind, trees, and bunkers to keep the golfer composed and focused on the shot. I heard caddies say things like, "OK, hit the ball smooth and clean," motivating the golfer to stay on track.

What does this all have to do with you? If these professional golfers need an advisor, no matter how money savvy you may consider yourself, everyone can use the outside perspective of someone who also knows the game intimately. Why would you not choose the right advisor to guide you through challenging times, keep you on track to accomplish your vision, and gain the outcomes you are looking for?

I have played golf with a caddy a few times in my life at courses that required it. The caddy would tell me to hit it to the right, and of course, I'd hit it to the left. He'd say, "Hit it left," and naturally, I'd hit it to the right. Around the fifth tee, I noticed that the caddy now understood how I actually play golf. They adjusted their advice based on my abilities.

I want you to find the right advisor to make sure that you do not fall into any traps that I have seen over and over and over again. A pro does not always play golf in seventy-two-degree weather with blue skies and no wind.

The question I pose to you: Do you want a transactional relationship with a financial institution—someone you don't know well who cleans your clubs and hands you a putter? Or do you want a relationship with an advisor who knows your goals and is guiding you through retirement, making sure you are aware of what you need to consider so you can enjoy this time in your life?

Advocacy: Beyond Knowing The Tools

Having someone who knows what tool to use—whether golf clubs or financial instruments—is just the beginning, at least the way I practice financial advisement.

Once, my wife, Smyrna, and I were thinking about remodeling our home.

Smyrna is a caring, genuine human being who balances me out much better than I could ever envision. I can't imagine anyone else tolerating me for this long because of how my brain works and my wiring, which is not all positive. We started dating in 1994, so I've known her for thirty-two years. Clearly, we have stuck together for a long time.

For the home remodel, Smyrna and I met with our interior decorator, who helped us interview three contractors. We were looking at the same scope of work with all three. Among the choices to be made were appliances. One of the contractors (spoiler alert: we did not choose him) said he'd order all of the appliances. So far, so good. Then he said, "Of course, I'll have to upcharge you."

I replied, "Well, you don't *need* to." The interior designer, Lauren, spoke up and told us she would order the appliances, no markup needed.

She understood. She was our advocate. I wanted someone to look out for me. I wanted to make sure that while my wife and I were not on-site, someone was looking out for what we were trying to accomplish. That's what Lauren provided for us.

In my work, I've always tried to practice advocacy on behalf of my clients and potential clients.

Early in my career, I worked with so many people who were just out to make the sale. The process was transactional and nothing more. I was determined to find another way. That's why my approach is advocacy. I want to give people the knowledge to make informed decisions. Maybe my services are a good fit, maybe not. But I am building a relationship of trust—of real advocacy—so if or when the time comes, people know I have their best interests in mind.

Becoming educated about the topics covered in this book is incredibly important as you navigate your way through your retirement years. The best chess players are lifelong learners. You should take the same approach to your financial literacy.

This book is influenced by my incredible clients, from whom I am always learning. Also, my thoughts and implementation have been influenced by Eugene Fama, the Nobel Prize–winning economist and Robert R. McCormick Distinguished Service Professor of Finance at the University of Chicago Booth School of Business. In a talk I listened to recently, Fama said, "There is always going to be noise. Your role as an advisor is to understand the person you are working with and help them think beyond the noise."

Politics creates noise. Feds raising or lowering interest rates creates noise. War, crime, and everything beyond your control creates noise that will distract you. My goal in this book is to make sure you understand that the noise does not mean you should dismantle everything. Sadly, that's exactly what happened to my father, which I will detail later in this book.

PART I

The Opening:
Avoid Financial Disasters

CHAPTER ONE

Why Your Story Matters When Planning For Retirement

The worst enemy of the strategist is the clock.
GRANDMASTER GARY KASPAROV

Do you have a plan A for retirement? Do you have a plan B? This book will educate you about both.

In many ways, this book is a love letter to my parents and their love of education. In my own way, I have become an educator. My mission is to educate families about the possibilities of a happy retirement.

Both of my parents focused their whole lives on education. My mother became a medical doctor in a time in Iraq when women didn't become doctors. She was not the type of lady who was just going to settle down and do what other people would tell her to do with her life. Education was her key to a better life. She went to Istanbul to attend medical school because she was not going to just settle and be a housewife. My mom bucked the system, which I loved.

My father grew up very poor. To escape poverty, he focused his attention on education. When we first came to the United States, he got his PhD, which demonstrated that, like a great chess player, he was planning way ahead.

Education was the plan A for my parents, but they always had a plan B to protect the family. When we returned from the United States to Iraq, and a war broke out with Iran, they put plan B into action. They had planned ahead, applied for my mother to get her PhD, and we ended up in Scotland. I have often reflected that these are the type of people who always thought out a plan B.

I've focused my whole career on understanding what it took for my parents to protect their family with their plan A and plan B. Their disciplined approach required a great deal of time, effort, focus, and attention to detail. To safeguard your retirement, the same is needed. This book is to help you with your plan A and your plan B.

Hardwired For Math

Often, people ask me how I got into this business. What made me jump into financial planning? The roots of my interest go back to childhood.

The interest started with chess, but I also see math in everything. For instance, I started playing snooker when I lived in England. It is similar to pool, but on a bigger table. There is a points system correlated to the color of the ball. So red is one point, black is seven points, pink is six, and so on.

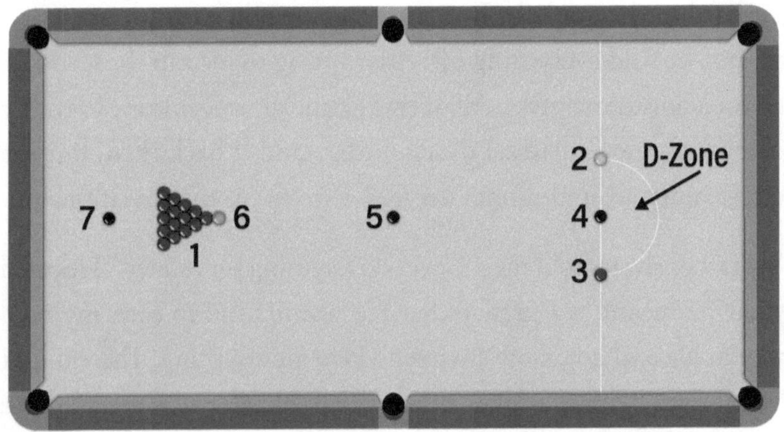

The idea is to read the table before hitting the colors and then try to get the most points. It's all math and angles. There is no grid, yet it all looked like a chessboard to me. I'm good at chess and snooker because I can see the math in my head. I am hardwired for it.

I can use math very quickly in my head. For instance, when I see someone who's age sixty-five, and they're spending $5,000 a month but only bringing in $4,000, and they've got X amount of dollars, I can reverse engineer in my brain, based on their age and everything else, how much extra they will need in retirement. Then I test the numbers with software and help them develop a plan to account for that $1,000 difference.

But I didn't just jump from chess straight into financial planning.

From Math To Financial Math

I was thirty-five when my father passed away. Part of his money story was how he tried to calculate the markets. In the 1980s, he got hit hard in the markets. In what I can see now as an overreaction to this, he sold everything off. Attempting to recoup those losses, he took additional risks. All of this financial stress meant I saw my parents argue regularly. I didn't understand it back then, but the uncertainty around money created a strain on their relationship.

My father always told me, "Never do anything for money." I learned what he meant as I grew older. He wanted me to earn my own way in life and not allow anyone to give me anything. There might be motives behind a "gift" down the road. This was great advice given by a very smart man. I've often wondered what might have been if he had an advisor to help him navigate after that big loss.

I started my career in banking, but did not find it fulfilling. It seemed to me that banks were limited in their ability to give advice to clients based on the client's total financial picture. It was often about promoting a specific product or course of action that would benefit the bank.

When I started my business, Safeguard Investment Advisory Group, I set out to take a different approach, one not geared toward products on a shelf. We're not focused on an agenda. At Safeguard, our role is to address the client's philosophy. One of the first things that we do is take a very in-depth approach to understanding who you are and how you relate to and feel about money, which is different for everyone. We don't want you to have our vision. We want to address yours.

Our second step is education. We want to educate you on where you stand today to see how that stacks up against your vision and goals.

The third step is to see if there's anything we can do to improve on what you've already accomplished and address that original vision.

So, I wanted to share with you my story of how I got started in the business and what I feel is so important when I advise people moving forward: It's their vision, not anyone else's.

Your Story Is Unique. Your Retirement Strategy Should Be Too.

Your story is important. You've worked hard all your life. Now, you deserve the independent retirement that can help you achieve your "happily ever after." At Safeguard, we work with all kinds of families and individuals, and we help each of them create a retirement strategy that fits their unique needs and lifestyle.

Our business model is simple: Our clients come first. When families and individuals place their trust in us, it's our job to help them make their dream retirement become a reality.

We understand how hard you've worked for your money, We're committed to working just as hard to help you thoughtfully manage risk and pursue your long-term financial goals through disciplined planning.

Understanding Your Backstory

We begin simply by listening to your life story up to this point— let's be honest, no one has gotten to exactly where you are in exactly the same way. It's your story we want to hear, and only by understanding where you've come from can we begin to understand your future financial goals.

Then, we provide a realistic assessment to help identify opportunities to enhance your existing retirement income strategy.

Here is my backstory from the last three decades.

Smyrna and I started dating back in 1994, which means we've been a part of each other's lives for more than thirty years now. In that time, we've built a life together, raising three remarkable kids: our daughter, Leena (twenty-three), and our sons, Yusef (twenty-six) and Adam (twenty-one).

Smyrna has always been the steady center of our family—calm where I can be restless, patient where I am driven. She's the balance to my chaos, the quiet strength that steadies our home. Honestly, she's the glue that holds us all together.

One memory always stands out when I think about how deeply I admire her. For years, every Saturday, Smyrna, the kids, and I would visit my mom and bring her lunch. My mom was a force—strong, healthy, a regular at the gym. Then, one day, what we thought were minor strokes changed everything. She came to stay with us for a few weeks while she recovered. Smyrna took her in without hesitation and cared for her like she was her own mother. My mom was most at ease in our home because of her—because Smyrna made her feel safe, seen, and loved.

But soon we learned it wasn't strokes after all. It was pancreatic cancer. Those weeks became precious, and near the end, my mom took Smyrna's hand and told her she was like a daughter to her. That moment touched something deep inside me.

Mom is gone now, but her influence lingers in all of us. I see it most clearly in our daughter, Leena—getting her doctorate in occupational therapy and, before long, will be called Dr. Abedeen. My mom inspired her.

Our sons, Yusef and Adam, are charting their own paths in the financial world, following the example they've seen at home. Yusef is drawn to the client-facing side of the business—he's the kind of person who lights up at a good math problem. He's learning every angle, positioning himself for the day he'll step into an advisory role. What sets him apart, though, isn't just his love for numbers; it's how easily he connects with people. He's poised, articulate, and genuine—qualities that make him a natural fit for leadership.

He plans to earn his CFP credential—Certified Financial Planner—a designation that demands the four e's: education, examination, experience, and ethics. It's a challenging road, but I have no doubt he'll excel.

Adam, meanwhile, gravitates toward the operational side of the business—the systems, the structure, the way things run behind the scenes. I can see him earning his CFP credential one day, too, not because he needs it, but because he's curious. He's already thinking beyond the day-to-day—about what kind of company we want Safeguard to become, what kind of culture we want to preserve. Even at twenty-one, he's got the mind of a businessman and the heart of a builder.

What I try to teach both my boys is simple: I don't care what you did yesterday. I care about what you're doing today, and where you're going tomorrow. That's the principle that guides me in business and in life. Understand how we got here, but don't stay here. Progress—that's another kind of mathematics. The formula for success isn't fixed; it's forward.

Writing Your Next Chapters

Every life tells a story. For many, retirement marks the beginning of a brand-new chapter—one filled with time, freedom, and the opportunity to live more intentionally than ever before. It's no secret that retirees today are living longer, fuller lives, and with that longevity comes both opportunity and responsibility.

We believe that financial independence isn't just about numbers on a page. It's about giving you the confidence to live the life you've worked so hard for—one where your income supports your needs, your goals, and the moments that matter most.

What Is A "Realistic Financial Review"?

When we talk about a realistic financial review, we're not referring to a quick glance at balances or rates of return. It's a process—one designed to bring clarity to your entire financial picture. Yes, it includes the traditional elements like rate of return, risk-and-reward analysis, and the creation of a tailored retirement strategy. But it goes deeper than that.

It begins by listening—by understanding your priorities and what matters most to you. From there, we look at how all the pieces of your financial life fit together and whether certain tools, such as insurance or other financial products, have been overlooked or underutilized. The goal is to identify opportunities you may not have seen before and bring them into alignment with your life's vision.

Beginning With You

No two people arrive at retirement in the same way. Your journey—your career path, your family, your triumphs and lessons—is as unique as your fingerprint. That's why we start with your story.

Our process is about showing you possibilities—different strategies and paths that could help you achieve your future goals. Our responsibility is to understand your financial world as completely as possible, then use our experience to ease your concerns and guide you toward a plan that brings both clarity and confidence.

Why It Matters

Most people don't realize how much the right tools can shape the quality of their retirement. Where you choose to place your hard-earned money affects not only your future income, but also how you experience it—from the taxes you'll owe on distributions and capital gains to how much of your Social Security income remains yours to enjoy.

When all the pieces work together, your financial plan becomes more than a strategy—it becomes a story of freedom, security, and purpose.

Measurable Results Without The Guesswork

Part of being hardwired for math means my work needs to be evidence-based. In mathematics, "QED" (an abbreviation of the

Latin phrase *quod erat demonstrandum*) is traditionally placed at the end of a proof to signify that the argument is complete and the statement has been rigorously demonstrated. The phrase translates to "that which was to be demonstrated" or "what was required to be shown."

Your previous financial strategy may have focused on the growth of your assets by adopting a "buy and hold" strategy, whereby you invested in the market and held onto those assets for an indefinite period of time before gains could be realized. Our process is much different. The time to achieve a measurable, quantifiable benefit is clearly defined using the math of insurance products and advisory services.

Understanding math, statistics, and angles has had the biggest impact on my life. This is knowledge that is constantly growing. Because you can't just learn math in one day, it's a gradual process. The same is true for financial strategies, which are really connected to math.

When you create a strategy, you have to calculate what the pitfall is. That's math. When I'm looking at someone's situation, I've learned to transfer myself into them by understanding them first. I don't do it immediately. I never assume anything.

Once I know who they are because of the process we develop, then I can almost transfer myself into their mindset. If things were to go wrong, what would the typical person like this do, and how would they react? That is a mathematical formula.

CHAPTER TWO

The Chess Game Plan To Avoid Retirement Mistakes (And Recover If They Happen)

*People who want to improve should take their
defeats as lessons, and endeavor to learn
what to avoid in the future.*
GRANDMASTER JOSÉ RAÚL CAPABLANCA

My father taught me the game of chess when I was just a young boy. I would want to play game after game, even though he would beat me every time. After several games and pestering him for just one more game, he would eventually have to carry on with adult stuff. While he went about his day, I would just stare at the chessboard. I was looking at all the angles, planning my attack, and determining how I could defend against his moves. That's how my brain has been wired ever since. I am eternally grateful for the time my father spent teaching me this game.

23

The number of possible chess positions is estimated to be between 10^{111} and 10^{123}, including illegal moves. If illegal moves are not considered, the number of possible positions drops to 1040. This number is known as the Shannon number, named after American mathematician Claude Shannon.[2] With so many options on the board at any given time, chess requires great focus. One of the biggest challenges is to remain focused and learn from mistakes when things go wrong.

Lessons From An International Childhood

I was born in Iraq to Dr. Mustafa Abedeen and Dr. Hikmat Alshaibi. They were very independent, successful in their professions, extremely smart, and calculating. My father was an educator. My mother was a medical doctor. After I was born, my parents, four sisters, and I moved briefly to the United States, where my father continued his education.

We lived in Nashville, Tennessee, during my kindergarten years while my father finished his doctorate at Peabody College. When Dad received his degree, we moved back to Iraq, where we lived in Basra. My father was hired as dean of a university there. I can still see him going to his beautiful office.

Iraq was not what it is today. The country was very modernized and growing. The economy was doing well because of oil.

My mother had her own medical clinic, and so the family was doing well. I remember going with my father as a youngster to Kuwait, and he would get a new car every few years. My parents were successful, and we had a good life.

My mother's will and desire to achieve something were always there. I often tell people I got lucky because I have my mom's business mentality with my father's calculating brain in one package. My mom and I often chatted about business. She always used to tell me that she's a business lady first because her clinic was first and foremost a business.

My father, being a dean of a university, did really well financially. He was respected and had many accolades and connections. I have a treasured picture of my father at the United Nations, part of an Iraqi delegation, because he had a PhD in English and education.

Those accolades and connections would become lifesaving for us.

Soon thereafter, a war broke out between Iran and Iraq. Basra is a town on the Iraqi border with Iran. I remember playing on the street, a street I can picture in my mind, and then hearing air raid sirens going off. We were always taught to go to the corner of the house as the safest spot during those frightening events.

Our house was positioned on a quiet street corner. I would hear the sirens and see what I now know were missile trails in the air. My sisters and I would go to that spot in the house where my parents had admonished us to go when the sirens were sounding. I can still hear those sirens.

Soon, the Iraqi government was conscripting young men into the army. My parents did not want this to be my fate, so once again we left Iraq. We packed what we could carry and headed to the train station. I was holding my father's hand. In his other hand was a briefcase. There was heavy security at the train station. As my father made his way through the crowd, the security personnel stopped him. I looked up, wondering what was happening.

What made me even more curious was what took place next. A higher-ranking officer saw what was happening and told the guard to let my father through. This kept occurring, "Let him go through, let him go through." My father told me later that there was money in the briefcase he was holding.

We were allowed to leave the country because my mother received a grant to get her PhD. For several years we lived in the United Kingdom, first in Scotland, then in England. I went to primary school in Glasgow, and then we moved to a town called Hull, in Yorkshire, England. I grew up there attending middle school, high school, and some college.

This experience of moving from place to place, from culture to culture—learning new languages and dialects along the way—has helped me approach life and the people around me with empathy. As language and culture were never a constant, math became my North Star. Wherever you go, two plus two will always equal four. The fundamentals of math are universal. The setup and rules of chess—my main pathway into the world of math—were consistent wherever in the world my family called home.

Early Lessons About Money

With no work visa, my father was not permitted to work in the UK, so he was living on his savings, and he started investing in the markets. He made sure his money grew prudently and had some success.

My father was a very methodical, calculating person. Markets were math problems. Then came the crash of 1987, when even the most calculating people were left with their guard down. We lost a lot, like many others during this time.

As a young child, I remember seeing my parents and hearing them fight constantly. Later in life I realized it had to do with money. My mother had her own money; my father had his own. They kept it separate. My father was investing for both of them. He made some knee-jerk reactions because his calculations did not work, and he did not stick to a systematic plan or stay disciplined in his reaction to things.

He had two very good, well-to-do friends who lived in the United States. They told him, "Mustafa, we have this investment that can make you a bigger return, and we will guarantee every penny of your money." Having made the wrong gambit after the crash, my father decided to trust these friends and attempt a bigger return to recoup what he lost. They went in together on a limited partnership. In the nineteen eighties, many such partnerships did very poorly. Many of them, including the partnership between my father and these American friends, went belly-up.

These friends were brothers who had promised him his money back. When things went wrong, this promise was not kept, and my father was left to pick up the pieces—another undeserved misfortune.

My Father's Hard Financial Lesson

What happened to my father should be a cautionary tale for us all about what occurs when emotion takes over from math.

If I could reverse time, I would share with my dad that when bad things happen financially, don't make a knee-jerk reaction. That was not the right move for him.

When he suffered the financial loss, he didn't understand the mathematical formula that caused his reaction to compound the troubles. He made the situation worse because his focal point became recapturing the loss. But the math had changed. He was no longer thinking logically. The moral of the story is that you lose sight of the math when you get emotional.

This bitter lesson has helped me extract the emotion out of my decision-making, which has helped me assist people by understanding them in order to best guide them in their situation. For my father, that lesson cost him more than money.

Having lost the money and with no way for my father to earn a living in England, my father and mother made plans to move to the States. Once we got our green cards, we moved here in 1990, and my dad started looking for work. He had a difficult time finding positions in his area of expertise, a professorship in English and education. He told me that he was overqualified, and I didn't understand what that meant at the time. But in telling me this story, he said, "If two people are applying for the same job and one is age thirty and the other is age fifty-five, they're going to hire the thirty-year-old because this person is going to seek tenure and stick around for decades."

Eventually, he found work teaching English as a second language. The damage done by that investment gone wrong never went away. It was psychologically holding him down because he no longer invested in anything. I see these challenges as major contributors to the health problems he developed over these years. The psychological damage and the fighting with my mother all took a heavy toll. In later years, he needed five bypass surgeries. He suffered multiple strokes afterward. He went through rehabilitation and recovered somewhat, but he was never the same.

Later in life, he never invested money. He relied instead on money market accounts and CDs. He became completely gun-shy and suspicious about any investment because of his past experience. My father could no longer trust his own judgment.

When I was around thirteen or so, I would hear my parents screaming at each other over money. My mother always had her own money. She didn't mingle it with my dad. That's how she was. As a kid, I don't think my mom ever gave me money. She was very frugal. I would tease her all the time. In my adult years, she wouldn't spend anything. She even recycled tea bags. So, when my dad lost this money, it was devastating for him, but it was a wreck for her.

When we moved to California, my Dad didn't want to buy a house. My mom said, "I don't care, we're buying a house. I'll buy it with what I have left." As a businesswoman, she knew the value of owning real estate.

Imagine somebody who left their country, who wasn't working, and now has to face another obstacle in their lives. They were not making much money, and they had to worry about paying to keep a roof over our heads. I think about that for someone who retires; it is no different. They have to make sure of the decisions they make, and they can't do it just on a whim. It has to be a mathematical calculation. Otherwise, it's an emotional decision.

Helping Others Navigate Life And Money

So, I understand, undeserved misfortune can strike anyone. The experience of watching my dad struggle so much is why I work so hard helping families avoid similar challenges. I see it over and over. People like my father, who work hard and do everything "right," have a bad experience, which blocks learning and evolving. Bad experiences with money can create even more hurdles to moving forward.

We've helped thousands of families. We serve through a disciplined approach rooted in education, integrity, and earned trust. My goal is for families who have worked their entire lives and done the right thing to have the life and retirement they envision.

The approach requires discipline, and I see the role of a financial advisor as being your champion when it comes to discipline. This approach requires continuing education for our advisors as well as our clients. If I want to advise my people to the best of my ability, I must live it, breathe it, and act it. I cannot be financially unstable and advise clients on how to become stable.

I received valuable gifts from my parents. My mother taught me the value of a business that serves people, and that a business needs to be profitable so it can stay in business to serve people. My father gave me two gifts: One was a love of chess, and the other was the importance of math and being able to calculate.

And now we help our families play retirement chess. We help them avoid mistakes. That's number one in chess: Don't make a mistake. But number two in chess is if I do make a mistake or my opponent makes a really good move, I need to be able to recover, have a new recourse, have a line of defense, and retake the offensive back. These are gifts that I use to help our families.

My mother said to me once, "It doesn't matter how much money you make. If you cannot put your head on the pillow at night and fall asleep, it means nothing."

A lesson I remember from my father was this: "Never do anything for money. You earn it. But be careful of the person who gives something to you. Be very careful."

Life will come at you with challenges. Economies lose steam. Markets rise and fall. As the world evolves, having a game plan that can be revised and evolve is crucial if we're to win the retirement game.

My Advice To Families

Let me end this chapter with my thoughts on legacy planning and the wishes, hopes, and dreams that families bring to us.

Retirement planning must be personalized. There is no one-size-fits-all, just like nothing in life should be. Inheritance is a gift, not a right. And I'm a firm believer in that.

For example, I helped an Egyptian woman whose husband died. They didn't have a true estate plan, but they had a property in Egypt.

The property didn't go to the wife, it went to the son. Now, that's not what the husband intended, but that's how things happen. So, I am a firm believer that a personalized plan should consider all aspects, whether you're giving it to the kids, others, or charity.

I don't think people should invest with the purpose of leaving their kids more. However, I think they should invest. And if they don't spend it, it should be a priority to make sure that the government and extra taxes are not in the picture. Because that's what not having a plan creates. That lack of design creates more money to go to the government for them to continue to waste, which is a problem for me.

Customization matters, and the discussion that creates that customization matters. Again, it is a mathematical formula. When I have a family that I'm helping, I always ask, "If you don't spend this all, where would you want it to go to?"

They might say "the children" or "a charity."

Then I say, "OK, let's talk about that and how we best position it."

PART II

The Middle Game:
The Safeguard Planning Playbook

CHAPTER THREE

Move #1:
Are You Taking Too Much Risk Or Is It Not Enough?

Some consider that when I play I am excessively cautious, but it seems to me that the question may be a different one. I try to avoid chance. Those who rely on chance should play cards or roulette. Chess is something quite different.

GRANDMASTER TIGRAN PETROSIAN

Managing money involves managing levels of risk. When people think about high risk, they tend to think about the markets. The stock market will move up and down. This will happen year in and year out, and you can never control when and how the market shifts. Something to keep in mind about the stock market: Bear markets will happen, but throughout the decades, broad stock markets have recovered from downturns over time. While the path and timing have varied, long-term investors have generally been rewarded for staying invested.

When managing risk, the question becomes, "What stage of life are you in?" There are three phases of our investment lives. There is the accumulation phase, where we can generally take the highest level of risk. There is the preservation phase, during which we're getting closer to retirement. And then there is the distribution phase, when we've retired and money from the first two stages works for us. This might be in the form of required minimum distributions or other funds to supplement Social Security to maintain the kind of life we want.

Understanding Inflation Risk Over Market Risk

Along with market risk, there is also inflation risk. If your assets are not appreciating over time, inflation will catch up, and your assets will not stretch as far in the future as they do today.

Here is where managing market risk is a helpful tool. I want you to consider that over time, the market will produce between 6 and 9 percent, as long as you are not withdrawing big percentages from it. Your growth and your market portfolio should be reinvested and allowed to compound. We've all heard the term "compounding interest" and how important it is. The challenge of letting your assets compound with interest: they must be left undisturbed. When markets go down, people tend to panic, and they sell, creating opportunities for cooler-headed investors to buy at discounts.

Instead of looking at when the markets drop, remember this: Every stock market in history has eventually recovered. Even during the Great Depression—one of the worst economic periods ever recorded—the market ultimately rebounded. From its peak in 1929 to its bottom in 1932, the market fell about 89percent. The market did ultimately return to and exceed its prior peak. The recovery took time, but history shows that markets have demonstrated resilience over long horizons.[3]

Should you be concerned about risk? Absolutely. The question to ask yourself: Do I have the right amount of risk at this stage of my life?

Are you in the accumulation phase where you could take a higher level of risk?

Or are you in the preservation phase where you're coming closer to retirement? This is when you do not want to take on too much risk and make mistakes.

As you enter different phases of life, you reduce your risk exposure, but you still have money working in growth.

Many long-term financial strategies include some exposure to the stock market because of its historical growth potential, though the right level of exposure looks different for every person.

There are two types of advisors out there. One will tell you that the market lost 50 percent during the 2008 crash. You don't want your money to lose 50 percent. And they'll tell you, "Put it all in fixed, maybe an annuity or CDs."

And the other type of financial advisor will say, "Look, the markets have risen over 100 percent over a period of years. Don't you want your money to grow 100 percent?" So, they'll push you in the other direction.

One of these will always be wrong. So rather than guessing, rather than making knee-jerk reactions, understand what stage of your investment life you're in and design it around that so that you do not make a mistake.

That is why educating clients is so important to me. If you know the market goes up and down over the course of a year, but has always trended up over time, you will not make a knee-jerk reaction. Find an investment advisor you trust and, in general, stay the course.

CHAPTER FOUR

Move #2:
Are You Factoring
In Taxation?

Help your pieces so they can help you.
GRANDMASTER PAUL MORPHY

Nobody loves to pay taxes, but they are a fact of life. Your biggest expense in retirement will likely be taxation. If you've been told you can eliminate taxes in retirement, that is a scam. There are ways to mitigate taxes, but you can't eliminate them altogether. There are only two paths for the government to get debt under control. One is to cut spending. Number two is to raise taxes. Let's not hold our breath for option number one to happen anytime soon.

As for option number two, the corporate tax cuts enacted under the 2017 Tax Cuts and Jobs Act are now permanent, or at the very least, they're going to be difficult to unwind. Therefore, the onus of taxation is on the consumer.

Taxes kind of sneak up on you. There is even a term for this: "stealth taxes." There are income-related monthly adjustment amounts (IRMAA) penalties, which are taxes on Medicare Parts B and D.[4] You pay Social Security taxes while working, and then they tax your benefits depending on your income in retirement. There are state taxes and local taxes. We are completely taxed to death. We're born free and taxed to death. We are taxed when we earn it, when we save it, when we spend it, and when we invest it. Then they tax us when we die.

Fortunately, there are ways to lessen the pain, but you must have a strategy for a tax-efficient work life and retirement.

Controlling Taxes On Investments

Is an investment making a good return when you need to give back a big chunk of that to the government? Something I always consider when investing is how we keep taxes under control. There are numerous approaches to this, depending on lifestyle, income, and whether you have a pension.

Your deductions are going to play a huge role in your future planning. With an ever-evolving tax code, it is crucial to have advisors who are on top of these changes. For instance, if you look at marginal tax rates over history, the top rate at one stage in the United States was 91 percent. Right now, it's 37 percent. These can be changed based on government policy.

The chess metaphor holds up well when it comes to thinking about taxes. You need to understand how the game plan is set so that you can make alternate moves. Typically, the federal government looks at the budget in ten-year increments. I believe they do this because, in ten years, the ballooning deficit and other issues will likely be someone else's problem. Who pays the price for this continual kicking of the can? You, the consumer. It is you and I who are going to pay the price for this. So, a tax approach to planning is a vital part of investing.

CHAPTER FIVE

Move #3:
How Much Are You Paying In Fees?

If you wait on luck to turn up,
life becomes very boring.
GRANDMASTER MIKHAIL TAL

The third big chess move is to understand investment fees. There are implicit and explicit fees for investing. Have you ever eaten at a restaurant? You get the bill, and you see that 3 percent was added to your bill. If you had examined the menu closely, you might have noticed, in tiny four-point font, a note about that 3 percent surcharge. Or when you've stayed at a hotel, and upon checkout, you notice a thirty-five-dollar-a-day resort fee that was added to your bill. Or, oh, you are buying a ticket to a concert, and the ticket price is advertised clear as day. But when you check out with your credit card, you notice several fees have been added to your charge. You then blink several times at a souvenir fee for a poster that you're going to get at the concert. What in the world is a souvenir fee?

The same is too often true with investment portfolio management. People are not given enough information, and they are surprised when they find out about these fees. Not being up front and transparent about financial services fees is unacceptable, in my opinion. This is the one thing that baffles me about the industry. Understand when investing—like everywhere else—there is no such thing as free.

How To Expose Those Fees

What should you be vigilant about regarding hidden fees? First, when you invest, you should consider expense ratios on the funds. Then there is what they call the "turnover ratio" within the fund, which is the number of times you buy and sell within the fund. Will expense and turnover ratios show up on a statement? No. That is something you have to read in the prospectus or research on Morningstar.

Depending on how high these fees are, they affect the overall return you get on the fund. I've seen funds that have had almost a 3 percent expense ratio, and the consumer was unaware. That means if the markets go up 6 percent, you'll end up with only a 3 percent gain. How does that make sense? You're taking all the risk and getting less of the reward.

An easy fee to find is an advisory fee. When you hire an investment advisor, you will see that the fee is disclosed in your statements. Fees can range from 0.6 percent to as high as 1.5 percent a year.

Most investments, like variable annuities, life insurance, and index annuities, have fees associated with them. Beware: Financial institutions have a very clever way to hide the word "fees." Look for terms like "participation rates," "caps," or "M and E (mortality and expense) charges." Understanding the internal costs of these investment instruments will help you determine whether the full cost is worth the returns you realize.

As mentioned above, in order to catch many of these costs, you'd have to read the prospectus. Here's a little life hack to find the information you are looking for in those long, boring documents: Read the footnotes and the endnotes in the prospectus. This is where the hidden disclosures are usually located.

Other fees to be aware of include revenue sharing, where brokerage firms are able to collect fees from mutual funds based on volume. Again, this is not going to show up on your statement. You'll need to Google it to find out if a firm is doing revenue sharing, and a lot of them do so through selling mutual funds.

One way to work around this fee is to choose a "no-load" fund. A no-load fund gives the investor the option to adjust at no additional cost if needed. There are no conflicts of interest, as there are no commissions, so if you do decide to sell it and buy something else, it will not cost you anything. Let's say I offered you Fund Family X because they were really good, and then two years later, I tell you, "Hey, Fund Family Y is better," and you look at the numbers, and they are better, but I tell you, "Well, it's going to cost you another commission." I just lost that opportunity because you have to pay commissions or additional transaction charges. This is not in the consumer's best interest.

Being aware of fees helps you calculate the real cost and real upside of an investment. Knowing what to look for and where to look for it equals more knowledge, which equals more power to you in the retirement chess game.

CHAPTER SIX

Move #4:
Are You Considering
Roth Conversions?

When you see a good move, look for a better one.
EMANUEL LASKER, GERMAN CHESS MASTER

There is no single chess move that will guarantee a win every time. In the world of personal finance, one strategy that can be especially powerful for certain people is converting IRAs to Roth IRAs. In fact, Roth IRAs and Roth conversions are tools that many people may want to evaluate as part of a thoughtful retirement and tax planning process.

Why is that? Before the answer, let's start with the mechanics of a retirement account. For those of you who have IRAs, 401(k)s, 403(b)s, or any type of pension retirement account, you enter an agreement—think of it as a business arrangement—with the US government. The IRS says, "Any money you put into these plans will grow tax deferred. We are going to give you immediate gratification in the form of a tax break when you place money into these accounts."

So far, so good. You get to place it into one of these accounts, and the government even trusts you to pick how the money is invested. The IRS says, "Listen, we are on your team. We want you to grow this money as much as humanly possible."

And you say, "Well, this sounds great. This business partnership is wonderful. What is your share?"

And the government says to you, "That's a great question, but don't worry about that right now." Let the alarm bells commence.

Or, let's say your brother-in-law comes to you because you can buy a piece of property from Grandpa, and Grandpa is going to sell you this piece of property, and your brother-in-law says, "Don't worry about it. I'll loan you the money, but I'll tell you what the loan rate is when we sell the property." Would you accept that deal? No. What if you had the opportunity to buy your brother-in-law out right now, and you knew what the terms were? If you could, you would do it because the future, while uncertain, is likely to cost more than the present.

Here is one more way to think about how the government approaches a traditional IRA. You've probably seen a TV show where the bad guys enter a mom-and-pop store and extort the owners for "protection" money. The bad guy boss always says something like, "You can pay me now, or you can pay me later," with the implication that the latter option will be more costly.

This is kind of how the US tax code works. "Tax deferred" does not mean "tax free." When you pay later, that comes at a cost. Why? Because it is based on a future rate at which the government will collect its portion of the money you invested. This number is, by definition, a moving target. With thirty-eight trillion dollars in debt currently, are we likely to see tax reductions or tax increases in the future? Tax rates do not tend to go down over time. If you've saved money and you have assets, you are not going to pay less later in taxes—unless you consider this approach and convert to a Roth IRA.

With any traditional IRA, if you remove funds prior to age fifty-nine and a half, you will pay the tax and also be hit with a 10 percent penalty. Up to this point, the IRS has been a helpful business partner in this venture. Now our partner says, "How dare you take money out of our joint venture here?"

When someone reaches age seventy-three, or age seventy-five if you were born after 1960, the traditional IRA becomes subject to required minimum distributions (RMDs). At that age, the government forces you to pull money out every single year, and those withdrawals are considered taxable income. The size of the RMDs increases at a certain percentage every year, and failure to withdraw the minimum amount results in severe penalties—not only is the tax still taken, but a penalty of up to 25 percent is assessed for that year's RMDs. If you let your IRA compound and grow, which we all want, your RMD is going to be higher, and if your RMD is going to be higher because your value went up, your taxes are going to go up as well.

I have a ninety-five-year-old client; her RMD is $250,000. She has to pull out 13 percent of all her IRAs. Never in a million years, when she was a librarian, did she think that she was going to pay 30-plus percent in federal taxes. She did what we are all encouraged to do. She invested, she has a pension, she has Social Security, and she's paying taxes on the whole thing at the highest rate. When it comes to IRAs, the government does not discriminate regarding age. Whether you are fifteen or ninety-five, they're going to tax you the exact same way.

With a Roth IRA, there are no RMDs. That is what makes a Roth or Roth conversion such an excellent move. You control how and when you take it. The only drawback: You cannot take a tax deduction on the yearly contribution.

How does a Roth conversion work? You can do it any time, but ideally, it is best to convert when markets are down. Let's say Apple stock is a part of your IRA, and it's worth $10,000, and it drops 30 percent, so now it's worth $7,000. That is an ideal time to convert to a Roth and pay the tax at $7,000. When the markets go back up, that money is there, and there are no required minimum distributions. A Roth puts you in control of when and how much you want to take out.

After a Roth conversion, the money needs to stay in the account for five years, but this is not bad news if this is money for the future and you have other liquid reserves available to you. If your vision is to have this money work for you in the future, you ought to consider making Roth conversions when it makes sense for your tax situation.

Under current tax law, qualified Roth IRA distributions are not subject to federal income tax and, in many cases, state income tax as well—though outcomes vary by individual situation, and tax rules can change over time. And while the day your beneficiaries inherit should not be the main criterion for choosing a Roth, it does offer a meaningful added benefit: It is tax-free to your beneficiaries, and once they inherit, they get to invest in it for ten years tax-free. There are also no RMDs for a Roth while the owner is alive, and qualified Roth withdrawals do not count as taxable income, which gives you another layer of control as you plan your retirement financial strategy.

Is It Time For A Pawn Swap?

As a child, I remember looking at the chessboard, just staring at it and searching for the best move. I forget what age I was when I learned about the pawn swap. In chess, when a pawn reaches the opposite end of the board, you are allowed to exchange it—"promote" it—for a more powerful piece. The most beneficial pawn swap is called "queening," when the pawn is exchanged for a queen of the same color. A pawn begins the game as the weakest piece, but if it stays on the board long enough and moves carefully, it can become the strongest piece you have.

Think of a Roth conversion as an advantageous pawn swap. The Roth conversion gives you so many advantages. In addition to tax-free withdrawals, because there are no RMDs, the money can continue to grow tax-free, and whatever is left can be passed along to your heirs. (Be aware that RMDs may kick in for your heirs after your passing.)[5]

As an immigrant, I love the opportunities the United States has provided me, and I learned that it is my duty to pay all the taxes that I owe, but not one penny more. It is not your patriotic duty to pay more taxes than you owe. There is nothing wrong with taking advantage of retirement instruments that help you avoid paying unnecessary taxes. The Roth IRA is a perfect example of paying your taxes but avoiding potentially higher taxes in the future.

Move #5: Do You Have An Income Separate From The Market?

Fame, I have already. Now I need the money.
WILHELM STEINITZ

In chess, if you can't anticipate what might happen several moves ahead, you are already losing. One never knows exactly what move your opponent will make next, but you can make educated guesses to game out how you will respond in different scenarios.

This is a good way to think about income planning. We can't predict the future, but we can make educated decisions based on what we know now. We can make decisions that help us manage uncertainty.

The economics and logistics of retirement have changed dramatically over the past century. On November 4, 1939, Ida May Fuller became the first person to draw from the recently formed Social

Security Administration. A few months after submitting her claim, on January 31, 1940, check number 00-000-001 was drafted in the amount of $22.54.[6]

Back then, life expectancy was around sixty-five years. The concept was that we pay into the system, as Ida did for a few years, and we would get this money back for as long as we lived. It was reasonable to assume that people could work until their mid-sixties and live comfortably for the few years they had left on Social Security plus whatever savings and pensions they might have from the one or two places they had worked in their lifetimes.

Today, life expectancy is much longer, and if you live to age sixty-five, you are actuarially likely to live a couple of decades beyond that age.[7] Pensions are much less common than they were when Social Security was in its infancy. And the math has changed dramatically, so Social Security should not be counted on as the main source of retirement income.

Albert Brooks wrote the novel *Twenty Thirty: The Real Story Of What Happens To America*. One question Brooks poses in the book: "What if we cure cancer?" That would be undeniably great news. It would also change things in ways it is difficult to anticipate. Longer life spans would have implications for healthcare, insurance, and the Social Security Administration. Any advances in medicine have the potential to change things. Keeping your game plan nimble is key.

There are always changes being made to Social Security. Sometimes they are minor tweaks. Sometimes major changes occur. For instance, the age of full eligibility for Social Security used to be sixty-five. As of this writing, full retirement age is sixty-six for those born in

1954 or earlier and gradually increases in two-month increments until it reaches age sixty-seven for anyone born in 1960 or later.[8]

Why is it important to have income that is not tied to the market? Markets are inherently volatile. A person who retires in a year when the stock market plunges has a much greater chance of running out of money than the person who retires when the markets go up. A foundation needs to be created outside of the markets.

While the stock market generally trends upward over time, one cannot rely on that upward movement day to day, week to week, or month to month. Say you work for a publicly traded company. During years when you are working for a paycheck, if the stock drops, your paycheck doesn't drop. And likewise, if the stock goes up, your paycheck doesn't go up.

When you retire, that regular paycheck is gone. Many retirees look to create more predictable sources of income designed to help cover their expenses, wants, and needs—much like a paycheck once did—while managing their exposure to the stock market.

An income separate from investments is a necessity. For those of you with pensions and Social Security, you may need less of this kind of income.

How do you know what you will need? We recommend doing a checklist of all your expenses and things on your list of things that "would be nice to have or do." With that in mind, you have a sense of how much of this will be covered by Social Security and any other reliable income sources you may have. The remainder should be invested in a way that allows it to compound and grow, and to support strategies such as Roth conversions when appropriate.

In a recent article, head of TIAA Institute Surya P. Kolluri is quoted as saying, "Instead of asking yourself how big a nest egg you need, think about how much annual income you need in retirement to maintain your lifestyle."[9] I've always said this: My role as a fiduciary, as an advisor, is not about adhering to my own philosophy. My job is to understand *your* philosophy and create an income plan based on that.

Three Buckets

Savings and investment should be placed into one of three buckets. Bucket one is your emergency fund. This money is set aside strictly for unexpected events, such as a job loss, medical emergencies, or major home or car repairs. Ideally, this bucket should hold six to twelve months of living expenses to ensure you can maintain financial stability even if your income is temporarily interrupted. The priority here is safety and liquidity, not growth.

The second bucket is your short-to-medium term savings. This bucket is designed for planned spending and lifestyle goals, such as vacations, large purchases, or temporarily supplementing your income. The focus is on accessibility and modest growth while preserving capital so the funds are available when you need them.

The third bucket is for long-term growth. This has market risk, but the point is to structure that risk so that once the other two buckets are filled, you can leverage these funds for growth over the long-term. Stocks and other investments can be volatile but tend to gain over time.

How do you manage these three buckets? Here's an example: Let's say you have a million dollars. Six months to a year of expenses would go into bucket one. Let's say that is $50,000, leaving $950,000. In one hypothetical scenario, a portion—such as $550,000 to $650,000—could be allocated to bucket three, the growth bucket. Depending on the investments used, these funds may remain liquid but are subject to market risk. Then, the second bucket is there for things you may want but are not daily expenses. For instance, if you want to take a nice trip to another part of the world, you use the money from bucket two because it's not compressed.

CHAPTER EIGHT

Move #6:
Do You Have A
Long-Term Care Plan?

*The biggest challenge is to fulfill
your own ideas about yourself.*
GRANDMASTER JUDIT POLGÁR

I f you're a baby boomer, the most famous chess match that comes to mind is probably Bobby Fischer versus Boris Spassky. Or you might remember IBM's Deep Blue versus Gary Kasparov. A more recent example is a match that the fictional character Beth Harmon plays against the Russian grandmaster in the Netflix limited series, *The Queen's Gambit.*

Most of us see chess as a one-on-one, *mono a mono* competition. But for many people, the game of retirement chess is a doubles match. It's you and your spouse—your partner—playing this game. The truth is, if you reach the age of sixty-five, there is a good chance that one out of two of you will suffer a major health issue before the game is over. How are you going to address that?

Because we are living longer, we are more likely to need long-term care. Many people think their health insurance or Medicare will cover their care in such situations. That is not the case. Long-term care is one of the most unfunded liabilities facing America.

I experienced this with my mother when she was diagnosed with pancreatic cancer. There came a point when the hospital could do nothing more for her. We faced the choice of placing her in a nursing home or paying for care in her own home. We chose in-home care and paid out of pocket. But not everybody has the ability to pay for care that way.

Think about what we've covered in the previous chapters. You can do all the right things. You can save, invest, pay less in taxes, and do a Roth conversion. But when a major health crisis occurs, all of that may not prepare you. The statistics show that as we age, the odds are that more than 50 percent of people need care at some stage of the game. That potentially puts all of your hard work and planning up for grabs and could devastate the surviving spouse's lifestyle moving forward.

What You Need To Know About Long-Term Care Planning

The first thing you need to know is how long-term care can affect your estate. When it comes to long-term care, there are certain assets that are going to be "attachable," meaning assets that will be expected to be liquidated to pay for long-term care. This includes all investment income and some pensions. The home will likely be exempt until passing, depending on the medical insurance. For somebody who has Alzheimer's or dementia, this could take ten to twenty years. I've seen estates completely wiped out because of the care needed for such a person.

How do you avoid this scenario? There are different ways to plan long-term care.

There are a lot of long-term care scams out there, so keep aware of that. In chapter 10, we will look at how to avoid scams geared toward people heading into or in retirement.

What Is Long-Term Care?

With so many misconceptions and assumptions surrounding long-term care, it's essential to be clear on what we mean by long-term care. Long-term care encompasses a variety of services that may require both medical and non-medical assistance.

Typically, long-term care is associated with any personal or medical assistance an individual may need to accomplish the activities of daily living, or ADLs.

These activities include things like bathing, dressing, continence and toileting, eating, transferring/moving from seated to standing, and getting in and out of bed.

When thinking of long-term care, people typically think of nursing homes and skilled nursing care. However, the majority of long-term care services are provided at home, in adult day health facilities, or in assisted living facilities.

Now let's look at four common long-term care myths.

Myth #1: "It Won't Happen To Me."

Few people want to face their own mortality, and it is human nature to think that bad things are more likely to happen to others than to oneself.

It's unsurprising that most people don't consider long-term care at all. In fact, a long-term care study conducted by AP-NORC at the University of Chicago found that, between 2013 and 2018, only about a third of those aged forty and older said they had set aside money to pay for long-term care expenses. And about half of those aged forty and older polled in 2017 and 2018 lacked confidence that they would have the financial resources to pay for the care they would need when they get older.[10]

Furthermore, according to the "Long-Term Care Marketing and Thought Leadership Research Survey" conducted by Versta Research on behalf of Lincoln Financial Group, only 14 percent of Americans discussed with a financial professional how they would pay for long-term care.[11]

Denial is powerful and can be detrimental in retirement planning. The reality is that whether you live a healthy or unhealthy lifestyle, chances are you'll need long-term care either way.

Myth #2: "Medicare, Medicaid, And Private Insurance Will Cover These Costs."

Many people think that health insurance, Medicare, or Medicaid will cover their long-term care needs. This is not the case.

Medicare doesn't provide long-term care coverage. In fact, Medicare typically only covers a portion of skilled nursing facility costs for up to one hundred days. A qualifying hospitalization must occur first to activate this benefit. Also, it provides only limited coverage for certain types of home care.

What about Medicaid? Medicaid only provides long-term care benefits to people with limited income and assets. If you are considering this option, you would need to spend down your assets—including real estate and investment income—to demonstrate financial need. Medicaid also has rules designed to protect the healthy spouse, which limit how much in total assets that spouse is allowed to keep and ensure they receive a minimum level of monthly income to live on. Spending down assets to meet these limits can also create tax exposure.

Employer-sponsored plans and private health insurance cover the same kinds of limited services as Medicare. If they offer long-term care services, it is typically only for skilled, short-term, and medically necessary care.

Myth #3: "I Plan To Self-Insure, So I'm Good."

Many people think they will be able to cover long-term care costs out of pocket. However, long-term care costs can cause people to draw down their savings much faster than anticipated.

You have worked hard to prepare for retirement, and, likely, you have spoken to a financial professional about a strategy. However, if a plan for long-term care hasn't been included, your retirement strategy is at risk.

Accessing funds to pay for insurance and long-term care costs can be taxable events, further reducing your retirement funds. Of course, there is the added stress that comes with trying to figure out how to pay for medical expenses while in a vulnerable situation.

Also, it is important to consider how an event like this would affect a healthy spouse. If all your retirement funds are being diverted to medical expenses, what is the remaining spouse going to use to live on? This is why it is essential to plan ahead.

Myth #4: "My Family Will Care For Me."

In past generations, spouses and children often took care of their loved ones when they were ill. It's easy to assume that family will care for a loved one's needs without considering the specifics. While millions of Americans do so today, it is crucial to assess the impact of providing care. If we set the financial burden aside for a moment, there are still many other considerations to weigh, such as the effect on careers, personal lives, and family dynamics.

It is also imperative to consider the full extent of providing or having care provided by a loved one. Consider the physical strain of lifting, bathing, and helping with activities of daily living. Is this something you are physically and emotionally prepared to do or have your spouse or child do for you?

What Are My Options For Long-Term Care?

There are several options for you to consider. Traditional long-term care insurance is designed to cover long-term services, including personal and custodial care in various settings such as your home, a community organization, or other facilities.

Touted as one of the most comprehensive resources available for long-term care, it is also the most expensive. Additionally, traditional long-term care policies have been plagued with premium increases stemming from the rising cost of healthcare affecting our nation. These policy premiums will likely continue to rise.

If you consider this route, understand that you must medically qualify for coverage, and if you can no longer afford the policy and cancel, you lose all the money you've put into it. Some people dislike traditional long-term care because of this "use it or lose it" provision. If you never need this type of protection, this is excellent news, but you do not get your paid premiums back in return.

Another option is annuities with long-term-care–related riders. Annuities tend to be much less expensive than stand-alone insurance, and some offer tax incentives for long-term care benefits. There are products available that allow you to take the premiums you'd pay for long-term care and apply them toward a fixed income while providing higher payouts should you require long-term care. If you don't need the benefits, the full value of the annuity can be used by you or your beneficiaries.

Typically, to receive these benefits, you must first spend down the full annuity contract value. There are usually additional fees associated with the purchase of this rider. Also, keep in mind that any withdrawals will reduce the long-term care benefits as well as the death benefit.

Next is life insurance with an accelerated death benefit, which can be used for qualified long-term care needs. If the insured needs qualifying in-home or nursing home care, they are able to receive accelerated benefits—meaning that they can pull the money from their life insurance policy for these expenses. This means the death benefits of the policy are reduced by what is received for long-term care coverage.

These policies provide multiple advantages: an income tax-free death benefit, income tax-free cash value, and the opportunity for an accelerated death benefit. You may have to medically qualify for coverage when the policy is issued, and there are usually additional premium requirements with the purchase of this additional rider.

Finally, one can opt for a life insurance/long-term care combo. This is a life insurance policy with long-term care benefits built into the policy, with an additional cost for these benefits. These products are typically more comprehensive than an accelerated benefit rider. You still have a tax-free death benefit and the opportunity to build cash value, along with the addition of long-term care benefits.

This type of solution typically involves separate underwriting for the life insurance and the long-term care protection, so it is possible to qualify for the life insurance but not for the long-term care benefit.

Planning for long-term care is analogous to a chess match. If you are too narrowly focused and don't plan well, you're going to leave room for life to deliver countermoves you are not prepared for. That's when your king could be quickly checkmated.

CHAPTER NINE

Move #7:
Are Loved Ones Accounted For?

In life, as in chess, forethought wins.
CHARLES BUXTON, FORMER BRITISH MP

We encourage our families to have candid conversations with their loved ones about their plans. One of my associates likes to say, "Don't fear the reaper, don't fear the planning, don't fear the conversations."

It's your money. You get to decide what to do with it. But it shouldn't be a mystery to your family after you're gone as to why you did things that you did. They shouldn't have to wonder why Mom or Dad made a specific financial decision that affects the family. Have those conversations.

For some people, that will be awkward, and there can be some discomfort with it. We understand. However, this will help families down the road. We sometimes see a sad thing with the passing of the main breadwinner. The spouse who is left behind gets a great deal of money, but they don't know what to do with it. They don't know who to trust. So, it's equally important that you and your spouse have a network of people you can both trust and go to.

While designed to provide valuable information, this material is not intended to offer specific legal or estate planning advice. Your unique situation will dictate the specific legal documents and strategies appropriate for your situation. Individuals are encouraged to consult with a qualified professional before making any decisions about their personal situation.

For many of us, the word "estate" conjures images of great wealth; we may mistakenly believe that the word belongs only to those with an abundance of wealth to be passed on to their heirs. But any adult who owns assets—young or old, married or unmarried, at any income level—is the keeper of an estate.

What happens to that estate when you die? It's an often uncomfortable but always important question. Estate planning involves creating a strategy for how those assets will be handled when you're no longer able to handle them. The process encompasses a range of tasks, from the creation of wills and trusts to preplanning for your funeral. A good estate plan can address a wide range of issues, including distribution of money, guardianship of minor or special-needs children, disposition of real estate, and more.

Many people don't have an estate plan in place because they perceive estate planning as time consuming and requiring lots of effort. And you're not required by law to have an estate plan in place; there are legal processes and procedures to distribute assets of individuals without directives in place.

However, establishing an estate plan communicates your wishes, outlining how you want your assets distributed and to whom. Your estate plan can also help protect your loved ones from having to make hard decisions about your health or your property when the time comes. It also helps your loved ones avoid the onerous task of untangling the details of your personal affairs.

One of the greatest gifts we can give to our loved ones is a plan of action for distributing or disposing of our assets after we die—allowing them to focus on healing and life after loss.

Will

The most basic tool in an estate plan is a will, a legal document providing instructions about how you wish for things to go after your death. A will can include a variety of things: It can express your wishes to divide all your belongings up among your living children or dictate that your grandmother's pearls go to your sister. Your will can outline whether you want your home to be sold or if you want your car to be donated. Your will can provide direction as to how all your "stuff" should be handled.

A will is also used by parents to express guardianship of a minor child or a child with special needs. Where will the child(ren) live? How will they be provided for? The will specifies your wishes about who cares for the kids if you're unable to do so. The person writing a will—the testator—chooses an executor, the individual who will be responsible for carrying out their final wishes. The executor is usually someone the testator trusts and who is at least generally familiar with the testator's affairs.

After the testator's death, the first step in taking care of the estate is to move the will into probate. During the probate period, the courts will determine if the will is authentic. If it's determined to be authentic and no one challenges the will's directives, the executor will begin the process of fulfilling the wishes expressed in the will.[12] While it is theoretically possible for you to write your own will, we strongly suggest that you use an experienced estate planning attorney.

Trust

A trust is a legal entity that can own assets or be named as a beneficiary for life insurance policies, IRAs, and other accounts. Like a will, a trust is set up with legal documentation, usually through an estate planning attorney.

There are two main types of trusts. The first type of trust, an irrevocable trust, cannot be modified or terminated without agreement from its beneficiaries, the people or entities that will ultimately receive the proceeds of the trust. The person(s) establishing the trust—the grantor(s)—can then shift ownership of their assets to the trust, removing the assets from their taxable estate. An irrevocable trust protects assets from creditors, since the assets are now owned by the trust and not by the grantor. [13]

The second type of trust, a revocable trust, is changeable as long as the person(s) who set it up—the grantor(s)—are still alive. With a revocable trust, grantors can receive income from the trust, but the assets are also included as part of their taxable estate and not protected from creditors. After the grantor dies, the revocable trust usually becomes irrevocable.[14]

As with a will, a trust also dictates how the grantor wishes for assets to be distributed and to whom they will be distributed. The grantor names a trustee, who is responsible for fulfilling the terms outlined in the trust documents. The trustee then distributes the assets of the trust to beneficiaries.

Probate is generally required when a decedent owns assets in his or her own name at death. The probate process transfers those assets to heirs. With a trust, probate is usually avoided when the trust owns the assets rather than the decedent.

A trust can be used in a variety of ways, including reducing the grantor's tax liability, preventing beneficiaries from misusing assets, or gifting a principal residence to grown children.[15] A trust can own life insurance or annuity policies and be its own beneficiary, either primary or contingent.

As a hypothetical example, the Joe Louis Revocable Trust is the owner of a life insurance policy, and Joe Louis is the insured. Joe would like his daughter to receive the proceeds of the life insurance policy directly, so he names her as the primary beneficiary. He names the Joe Louis Revocable Trust as the contingent beneficiary—in the event his daughter is unable to receive the benefits. Then the trustee can distribute proceeds from the life insurance policy as the trust directs.

A trust and a will can help reduce family drama after a death. They outline your specific wishes, helping your loved ones avoid making tough decisions guessing at what you wanted. If you suspect there may be drama, such as children fighting over who gets what, naming an impartial third party to be the trustee may be a good choice.

Legal documentation for wills and trusts should be completed by a qualified estate planning attorney. Your financial professional can help you identify which assets should be moved into the trust and how to register them correctly. They can also work with your lawyer to verify your account paperwork matches up with the trust or will documentation, double-checking the details now to help ensure your heirs avoid a messy situation later.

A Durable Future

A durable power of attorney (DPOA) is a legal document that allows you to designate another person (your agent) to make financial and legal decisions on your behalf in the event you become incapacitated or unable to make decisions independently.

Upon execution, your agent gains the authority to manage various financial matters, such as banking, investment decisions, real estate transactions, and bill payments. Additionally, they can handle legal matters like signing contracts, filing tax returns, and managing business affairs, depending on the scope defined in the DPOA document.

It's important to note that while the person designated in your DPOA to act on your behalf can also serve as your trustee or executor, these roles entail different responsibilities. Therefore, it is wise to carefully consider whether the same individual should fulfill all these positions or if different people may be better suited for each role. Choosing the right DPOA agent requires careful consideration. The agent should be someone trustworthy, responsible, and capable of making sound decisions that are in your best interests. Without this critical estate planning document, your loved ones may have to navigate complex legal processes, like guardianship or conservatorship, to manage your affairs. These processes can be costly and time-consuming and may not necessarily align with your preferences.

Make It Official

Establishing a will or a trust doesn't mean that all your assets are guaranteed to be distributed at your death in the way you intend. Sometimes assets pass automatically at death because of the way they are titled—joint tenancy with right of survivorship as a hypothetical example. A will would have no effect on such assets. Other kinds of assets—such as life insurance or annuities—have beneficiary designations. Those designations supersede the instructions of a will or trust.

Here's a hypothetical example: Say that Donna is the owner of a life insurance policy she established when she was married to her now ex-husband, Jack. Donna was required to keep insurance on her life as part of the divorce settlement, and Jack was required to be the beneficiary. The purpose of the life insurance was for Jack to take care of the kids while they were young.

Now, assume Donna's youngest child had just turned twenty-two when Donna died unexpectedly. Unless she changed her beneficiary designation before her death, the proceeds of the policy will probably still be paid to Jack, even though her kids are grown. This is a potential result, even if Donna's will states she wants all assets split equally among her kids.

If assets are being moved into a trust, ownership paperwork will also need to be updated to reflect the name of the trust as the new owner. Neglecting to update either ownership or beneficiaries on accounts intended to be paid out to trusts can create a massive headache—and unintended consequences—for your heirs.

Your financial and legal professionals can help you identify which assets are available to move into the trust and which ones need to be updated for new beneficiaries, as well as assist you with obtaining and completing paperwork for the necessary changes.

Healthcare Directive

An advance healthcare directive, also known as a living will or healthcare power of attorney, allows you to express your medical treatment preferences even if you are unable to communicate or make decisions independently. This document outlines your choices for medical interventions, life-sustaining treatments, pain management, and end-of-life care.

In this legal document, you appoint a healthcare agent or proxy: a trusted individual who will act as your advocate and make medical decisions on your behalf. Your healthcare agent will ensure that healthcare providers follow your expressed wishes and make decisions in alignment with your values and beliefs.

Without a clear and legally binding healthcare directive, medical decisions may fall to family members or medical professionals who may not be aware of your preferences. This can lead to unnecessary stress and confusion during critical medical situations.

Choosing a healthcare agent is a significant decision. Your agent should be someone who understands your values, is willing to uphold your wishes, and can effectively communicate with medical professionals on your behalf.

CHAPTER TEN

Move #8:
Have You Protected Yourself From The Scammers And Identity Thieves?

*No false move should ever be made . . .
to gain an advantage. There can be no
pleasure in playing with a person
once detected in such unfair practices.*
BENJAMIN FRANKLIN IN *MORALS OF CHESS*

Have you recently received a notification that there's been a data breach and that your information is now on the dark web? Almost every American has received multiple notifications like this. Our information is compromised. One rule of thumb is to change your toothbrush and your password every thirty days.

At a recent conference I attended, John Iannarelli, author and former head of cybercrime for the FBI, used the meeting room wi-fi to see what he could find about himself. He was able to find information like his Social Security number, account codes, and other sensitive data. Of course, he knew where to look, but was making the point that criminals also know where to look. We live in a world in which we need to protect ourselves.

In my twenty-plus-year career, I've had interactions with a few clients who have been scammed or suffered a scam attempt. They might buy investments like my father did in limited partnerships or something inappropriate. I've been able to get two people their money back.

One was a woman who, at the end of 2000, invested in a place called Yucatan Resorts. I got wind of it, researched the "company," and found out it was a scam when I tried to contact them. I couldn't sleep at night. I knew they were taking advantage of her. Finally, I called Yucatan Resorts and posed as her son. I said, "Listen, I understand the situation. I know what you are doing. You give my mom her money back, and I won't take this any further."

They sent her money back. The Yucatan Resort went out of business a few months later. Without someone intervening in such a way, my client would have been in the same position as my father. She remained a client for the rest of her life.

In another instance, I noticed a client had begun liquidating some accounts. I reached out and asked, "Hey, is everything OK?" They said, "Yes. Don't worry about it. I just have to make some repairs on the house." But something just seemed off about the situation. I called the client again, and they finally shared that their identity had been stolen. The scammers gave the impression that the Federal

Trade Commission was helping protect the client's identity, and the money would be put into an electronic vault.

We are all potential scam targets. It happened to me recently. I came home from vacation and found a check from the US Department of the Treasury. It was odd to me. I called the next day and asked what the check was for. They told me that it was my tax refund. When I asked for what year, they told me it was last year's return. I hadn't yet filed my tax return.

The Department of the Treasury found that a CPA in Roseville, California, had filed the return. That's not where my CPA is located. Someone had gotten hold of my W2 and my Social Security number and filed a tax return for me and my son, Adam. All of this could have been avoided if I had had an IP PIN on file with the Internal Revenue Service, which everyone should have today. This way, no tax return can be filed electronically without this PIN.

Develop An Identity Theft Plan

There are other similar stories taking place as I write this. Suffice it to say, if we can help clients avoid scammers, we do everything we can. With identity theft becoming more advanced, scam artists are constantly looking for ways to manipulate and take advantage of people. I would be in violation, in my opinion, of my fiduciary obligation if I did not make people aware of this.

What can you do to put an identity theft plan in place? In addition to using identity theft protection software and shredding sensitive documents, everyone should consider freezing their credit. Just go online to any of the big three credit bureaus and freeze it. When you are ready to apply for a loan, you can unfreeze it instantly. This will protect you from anyone taking advantage of your Social Security number.

The second thing is to have an IP PIN on file with the IRS. Also, make sure to have an organized, safe place where all your credit card information is, so that if your identity is stolen, you can contact these creditors instantly to protect yourself. It is important to be proactive and take these measures in advance.

Remember, government entities like the Social Security Administration, Internal Revenue Service, or the Federal Trade Commission will not call you. They will send you certified mail. Anyone calling and claiming to be from these organizations is not on the up and up.

A scammer is like the unscrupulous chess opponent Ben Franklin warns us about. Your chess opponent is very sophisticated. They study you.

I knew an attorney who once lost $700,000, thinking he was helping the federal government. A sophisticated, intelligent person fell for this. This $700,000 loss was a double whammy because the attorney still owed the IRS the tax money they had handed over to the scammer. There's no way for the government to forgive this because they can't know if you took the money out and put it on "red" at a Las Vegas roulette wheel or if it went to a scammer. This was a terrible situation. Not only did the attorney and spouse lose their nest egg, but they wound up deep in debt to the government for this. The IRS is sympathetic, but there's nothing they can legally do to help you.

Identity theft continues to rise each year, with more than 5.4 million fraud and identity-theft reports filed in 2023 and over $10 billion in consumer losses.

Common tactics identity thieves use include:

- Phishing and smishing: Fake emails or texts asking you to verify account information.
- Dumpster diving: Stealing account statements or Social Security numbers from trash or mail.
- Wireless hacking: Capturing personal information over public or unsecured wi-fi.
- Scams and false offers: Fake lotteries, job ads, or promotions meant to lure personal details.
- Shoulder surfing: Watching or listening to capture your PINs or payment information.

Ways to protect yourself:

- Shred sensitive documents before discarding them.
- Avoid online banking on public wi-fi.
- Create strong, unique passwords and update them if a breach occurs.
- Check bank and credit card statements regularly.
- Review your credit report annually and freeze your credit if necessary.
- Keep your home network secure and use virus-detection software.
- Collect mail daily or place a hold when traveling.

> If your identity is stolen:
>> Report it immediately at IdentityTheft.gov or by calling 877-IDTHEFT. You may also need to file a report with your local police department.[16]

One thing I'll add is that the government is inundated with all of this. The FBI and Federal Trade Commission are working hard to combat these challenges, and new legislation to combat cybercrime and other forms of scamming is constantly being introduced in Congress.

If you are the victim of a scam, it can be devastating. However, you have to recover and move on. You can't quit the game. You have to find a way to keep playing and find a way out, and that's why your financial advisor is there to help you.

PART III

The End Game

In order to improve your game, you must study the endgame before everything else, for whereas the endings can be studied and mastered by themselves, the middle game and the opening must be studied in relation to the endgame.

GRANDMASTER JOSÉ RAÚL CAPABLANCA

CHAPTER ELEVEN

Move #9:
Financial Plans Are Not
"Set It And Forget It"

*One thing which has been very important
to my success is my mental mindset.*
GRANDMASTER HOU YIFAN

You may recall the infomercial in the early 2000s: the Ronco Showtime Rotisserie. "You just set it and forget it," the pitchman exclaims. That may work on rotisserie chickens (or rib roasts with the included attachments). It does not work on life planning, and it definitely does not work in financial planning.

Think how your lifestyle has changed throughout your life. When we are young, we might drive fast, and as we get older, we slow down and pace ourselves. We have different interests and priorities at different points in our lives.

Similarly, a financial plan is not once and done. Your plan created today will not remain the same for the rest of your life. It should be updated as children come along, as jobs and income change. There will always be a need to learn new chess moves. You still need to look at the chessboard and make sure you're seeing all the angles as your personal economics shift in relation to larger economic factors.

Tax laws are changing; life expectancy is changing. Technological change is a constant. Opportunities are going to change. You may have investments that shouldn't be in your portfolio five to ten years from now because the cost of living is changing.

How are you supposed to manage all of this? Who has time to think, adjust, predict, and react? The first step is to set up what we call a strategy meeting. Whether you're working with an advisor or you're studying on your own, a strategy meeting is about looking ahead.

A strategy meeting is different from a review. Many times, I see advisors doing a review, only looking backward. Now, if I look backward and I am walking forward, I'm going to hit a wall or some other obstacle. Ouch.

Please don't misunderstand me: Looking back is essential. We need to recall and understand what happened in the past, but our actions cannot be based solely on the past—they must be thought ahead. So, in strategy meetings, you're always looking ahead, not the other way around.

A Good Outcome Starts With A Good Process

Early in my career, I worked for a financial advisor whose clients did not like to see him coming. They always thought he had something to sell them. That's the only time he showed up.

I asked him if I could take over the meetings with the existing clients, and I developed a system to review their financial situation. It was based on asking them about their values, asking them about their goals, and showing them which policy or product they had purchased was working toward that and which wasn't serving them anymore. And would they like to know other ideas that would serve their plan?

Not only did the satisfaction level go up, but I know we also helped so many families with what they really wanted in life.

I developed a process for a strategy meeting, or series of meetings, that would help me educate clients on their current financial situation and what their ideal future looks like. In the process, I would come to understand who they are and how they think about and relate to money. Not all of us think and relate to money the same.

The next step would be to create congruence. If where they are and where they want to be are out of sync, I proceeded to share ideas that could bring that hoped for future closer to reality. Rather than a transactional approach, I was bringing a strategy that focused on who the client is and what they wanted from their financial future. This changes the whole picture because now I am focused on their vision.

Later in my career, I was asked to educate other advisors on how to develop this process so they could better serve the families they assisted.

As a business owner, what you measure matters. So, if you measure things strictly in dollars, then only dollars matter to you. If you measure against your purpose of helping families, that creates different behaviors and different ways of doing business.

The point is, the process I have developed helps people look at their current situation, understand how they view money, and be nimbler in making changes as life happens and situations change. A transactional, set-it-and-forget-it approach does not leave room for adaptation. And we all know, life is adaptation.

CHAPTER TWELVE

Move #12:
Monitor Financial Future Trends

*Critical thinking is the most important factor
with chess. As it is in life, you need to think
before you make decisions.*

GRANDMASTER HIKARU NAKAMURA

've always thought of myself as a student of the game of chess. Likewise, keeping my education up and constantly reading and reviewing my work like I would study a chess board is vital for not only my success, but the success of my clients.

Like the game of chess, monitoring financial trends is not about reacting to every new piece of information that comes along. It is about discerning whether or how that information relates to the moves you have been making up to this point. And finding the latest TikTok influencer's sixty-second guide to living like the ultrawealthy is not the same as keeping your eyes open for solid information and opportunity.

The main reason I wrote this book is to help people become informed consumers, so you are not buying things just because the grass appears to be greener on the other side. When working with a financial advisor, be aware of how transactions are generated, understand advisory fees, ask questions, and find out where the conflicts of interest might be lurking.

There will always be noise to distract us from what is important. I was watching a documentary called *Tune Out The Noise* about Professor Eugene Fama, a Nobel Prize-winning economist, and others from the University of Chicago. One of the things that resonated with me, he said, "There's always going to be noise. Your role as an advisor is to understand the taste of the person you are helping." Politics is going to create noise. War, crime, and everything else are going to create noise that will distract you. My goal in this book is to make sure you understand that the noise does not mean you should dismantle everything. That's exactly what happened to my father.

In Ecclesiastes 7:12, King Solomon writes, "Wisdom is a shelter as money is a shelter, but the advantage of knowledge is this: Wisdom preserves those who have it."

We're not just protecting our assets; we're investing in wisdom to safeguard our future and the futures of our children and grandchildren. It pays to stay up on trends. How will AI and other technologies affect the way we live and invest? Will the Fed raise interest rates? Will they lower interest rates? Will there be new taxation from Washington? Will there be advances in healthcare that change life expectancies? All we know for certain is that there will be change, and you need to be a student of change.

I hope that we meet one day, and if we do, I hope that you share with me that there was some wisdom you gained from this book that improved your situation. And if we do meet and I can be of any further assistance, or if anyone on my team can, I would welcome that opportunity.

So, best wishes, and may the odds of the chess game be in your favor.

The Gen X Factor

For Generation X, the 1994 film *Reality Bites* is a cultural touchstone.

When it comes to financial anxiety about retirement, the film's title captures the feelings of many Gen Xers.

Reality Bites was Ben Stiller's directorial debut and explored themes of identity, compromise, and the disillusionment often felt by Gen X. Characters like Lelaina, played by Winona Ryder, and Troy, played by Ethan Hawke, represented different facets of Gen X's attitudes toward work and life.

Gen X is the demographic cohort born roughly between 1965 and 1980, following the baby boomers and preceding the millennials. The elder Gen Xers are approaching or reaching retirement age.

Gen X is known for being independent and adaptable, as they were the first to grow up with personal computers and witnessed the transition from analog to digital technology.

They are often referred to as the "middle child" generation because they are smaller than the baby boomers and millennials.

When it comes to retirement, Gen X is caught in the middle. And they are feeling the squeeze.

Gen X has always had to be more independent. Many Gen Xers are naturally suspicious, cynical, and doubtful. There is nothing wrong with questioning, because questioning will help you calculate the mathematical formulas to safeguard your retirement.

Why Reality Still Bites

Generation X is struggling with inflation, according to a 2025 Allianz Life survey. Seven in ten Gen Xers say inflation has hampered their savings.[17] Eight in ten worry they might not be able to afford the retirement lifestyle they want because of rising costs.

Daniel de Visé, writing in USA Today, summed up their plight when he wrote, "For Generation X, retirement beckons. And reality still bites." Here is his take on what Gen X is facing:[18]

> *A raft of new surveys suggests the MTV Generation is regretful about past financial missteps, anxious about the current economy, and fretful about the future.*
>
> *Many Gen Xers sense they haven't saved nearly enough to fund a comfortable retirement. They wish they had started saving sooner. They fear outliving their savings.*
>
> *Gen Xers also worry the stock market is about to crash, a scenario with which they are all too familiar, having survived the Great Recession of 2008 . . .*

It's a generation largely defined by financial uncertainty. Generation X was the first to cope without ubiquitous workplace pensions, relying instead on a new savings tool called the 401(k). The Great Recession stands as the generation's defining economic event . . .

Gen Xers believe they will need $1.6 million to retire in comfort, according to [Northwestern Mutual's] 2025 Planning & Progress Study. That's higher than the retirement "magic number" for other Americans.

But most in Generation X don't have nearly that much saved. A majority report having no more than two or three times their annual income in retirement savings.

By talking to Gen Xers, I understand why more than half of them think they will outlive their savings. This is not an irrational fear because Americans are living longer. By contrast, only about 40 percent of boomers fear running out of money in retirement.[19]

So, Gen Xers don't see themselves as kicking back on the porch with a beverage, taking it easy during their golden years. This is why nearly half of Gen X plans to continue working in retirement, generally out of necessity.[20]

Something alarming from research data, according to Northwestern Mutual, as discussed in de Visé's article, is that not enough Gen Xers have formal retirement plans. Only one-third of survey respondents said they are working with a financial advisor.[21]

Gen X has every right to be skeptical and suspicious. There are too many bad actors in the financial services industry. The Bernie Madoffs didn't make our lives as financial advisors any easier.

Retirement Is No Time To Go It Alone

In my view, Generation X has struggled more than other age groups to recover from the Great Recession. Every generation suffered in 2008, but economic research suggests Gen X suffered more than most. Add to that, the long-term effects of the pandemic have hit Gen X hard. This is especially true in the workplace, leading to job loss and uncertainty.

Many in Gen X have been forced to do independent thinking their whole lives. But retirement is a once-in-a-lifetime challenge, and it pays to get someone you trust to help with the math.

For Gen X, Safeguard Investment is determined not to pitch or promote products without first understanding the person. We do not believe in templated, cookie-cutter plans and standard recommendations for all.

Instead, we need to understand who they are, how they think about money, how they relate to it, and what truly matters most to them. We ask intentional questions that help our advisors provide the best possible guidance for their unique situation.

Once we know what a family really wants, then we do the math—and just like in school, we show our work. Educating families on the math behind decisions is one of our core beliefs.

Whoever you choose to work with, you should expect this same level of care and curiosity.

It's not a transaction. We're hired to advise and guide families, not to sell products or a fund. That's what we do—that's the focus at Safeguard Investment Advisory Group.

Appendix

Acknowledgments

The creation of this book has been more than a decade in the making, and it would not exist without the guidance, support, and belief of many extraordinary people.

First and foremost, to my beautiful wife, Smyrna. You are the cornerstone of our family. Thank you for believing in me, inspiring me, and being the most extraordinary mother to our three amazing children. Nothing in my life would be possible without you.

To Yusef, Leena, and Adam—you are the reason I do what I do. Watching the people you are becoming fills me with pride beyond words. You will change lives and make this world better. Thank you for teaching me more than I could ever teach you. I love you.

To my parents, Dr. Mustafa Abedeen and Dr. Hikmat Alshaibi. Thank you for your strength, your sacrifices, and the belief you placed in me long before I could understand its depth. You taught me to work hard, think deeply, and face adversity with courage. My career, this book, and the life I've built are all possible because of your love and example.

To my dear friend and mentor, Bill Kentling. Thank you for pushing me, for refusing to let me abandon this project, and for challenging me to dig deeper into my story. You have made me a better leader and a better advisor for the families we serve.

To one of my greatest friends, Josh Whitehead. Thank you for your honesty, your calm voice of reason, and for always answering the phone—no matter what you had going on. Your friendship means the world to me.

To Julie Scott and Loretta Murray, who have been here from the very beginning. Your sacrifices, your belief in what Safeguard could become, and your loyalty have shaped this firm from day one. You are the glue that holds so much together, and we would not be who we are without you.

To our loyal and dedicated operations team—Purple Salerno, Kelly Torres, Katty Flores, Thannia Gonzalez, and every member of our team. You are the backbone of this company. Thank you for treating our clients like family and consistently going above and beyond. Your excellence sets the standard.

To Kerrilyn Collins, whose creativity, belief in this project, and unwavering commitment helped bring this book across the finish line. Thank you for guiding our team forward, elevating our work, and helping me tell this story the way it deserved to be told. You pushed me to complete this book and believed in it even when I had doubts. Your encouragement—in this project and in every area—has made all the difference.

To our advisors, the team that made this possible—my partners Rick Rivera and Eddie Sota, as well as James Murray, Chris Miller, Andy Anable, Jon Magoch, and Deryk Cherubini. Thank you for your trust, your integrity, and your commitment to doing what's right—even when it's not easy. You are the future of Safeguard, and your impact on our clients and our firm is immeasurable.

To Cody Foster and David Callanan, and the Advisors Excel team. Thank you for your support, your guidance, and the countless ways you've helped elevate Safeguard. Your leadership and partnership have played an important role in our continued growth.

To Henry DeVries, whose editorial insight, steady guidance, and encouragement were instrumental in shaping this manuscript. Thank you for helping me tell my story with clarity, authenticity, and integrity—and for giving me the space and confidence to tell it my way. This book would not have been possible without you and your dedicated team.

To everyone who believed in me and in the mission of Safeguard: thank you. This book is a reflection of the work we have done together and the families we have the privilege to serve.

APPENDIX B

About The Author

Reid Abedeen is the managing partner at Safeguard Investment Advisory Group, LLC. He has helped retirees for over twenty years with issues such as insurance, long-term care planning, financial services, asset protection, and many other areas.

Upon receiving his degree in business administration, he began the first leg of his career in the banking industry. Always looking for ways to help clients, Reid realized that institutions were limited in the personal assistance that they could offer families. Believing that clients and their families should come first, he decided to go on his own in order to give the proper help and guidance that many families need in determining their retirement goals.

As an investment advisor, Reid's primary focus is to get a complete picture and understanding of what each client is looking to achieve personally and financially, as well as with estate planning for their heirs. Additionally, a plan of action does not mean forcing ideas on a client, but assuring the plan they have in place is sound and on track to meet those goals and objectives. Reid believes every individual should be well-informed about retirement options.

He shares his knowledge and experience as a regular contributor to Kiplinger and can be heard on the radio in San Diego on KCBQ The Answer and AM590 in Riverside.

APPENDIX C

Further Resources

Take Charge Of Your Taxes

Tax law adjustments each year prompt taxpayers to revisit their financial plans, but this year's changes could be particularly impactful.

The One, Big, Beautiful Bill Act significantly affects federal taxes, credits, and deductions. It was signed into law on July 4, 2025, as Public Law 119-21. The law aims to make the 2017 TCJA tax cuts permanent while reducing taxes for working families. Here are key provisions:

Individual Tax Relief: Average family of four making less than $100,000 may receive a $600 tax cut, with some estimates suggesting up to $10,900 in additional take-home pay.

Family & Education: Child Tax Credit boosted to $2,200 per child.

SALT Deduction Cap: Increased from $10,000 to $40,000 (effective through 2029).

Senior Benefits: Additional deduction of $6,000 per senior (age 65+) for 2025–2028.

Auto Loan Interest: Potential deduction of up to $10,000 for interest on US-assembled vehicles.

Estate Tax: Exemption increased to $15 million per person.

Business Taxes: Makes R&D and equipment expensing permanent.

Standard Deduction: Increased for 2025 to $15,750 for single filers and $31,500 for joint filers.

No Tax on Tips/Overtime: Temporarily eliminates tax on tip income (up to $25,000) and overtime pay (up to $12,500/$25,000) for 2025–2028.

President Donald J. Trump faces a formidable fiscal challenge. During his term, the national debt is projected to reach unprecedented levels, already exceeding federal spending on defense and senior health care.

For more details, visit https://www.irs.gov/newsroom/one-big-beautiful-bill-provisions

TAX RATE	**2026 TAX BRACKETS**	
	For Single Individuals, Taxable Income	*For Married Individuals Filing Joint Returns, Taxable Income*
10%	Up to $12,400	Up to $24,800
12%	$12,401 to $50,400	$24,801 to $100,800
22%	$50,401 to $105,700	$100,801 to $211,400
24%	$105,701 to $201,775	$211,401 to $403,500
32%	$201,776 to $256,225	$403,551 to $512,450
35%	$256,226 to $640,600	$512,451 to $768,700
37%	$640,601 or more	$768,701 or more

Our tax system is progressive, so the more you make, the higher the tax rate on each block of subsequently higher income. In other words, even if your total income falls in a higher tax bracket, you won't pay that rate on all of your income. For example, a single person earning $260,000 in 2026 would pay the following rates (assuming there are no adjustments for deductions, credits, etc.):

10% on the first $12,400	=	$1,240
12% on the next $38,000 ($12,401 – $50,400)	=	$4,560
22% on the next $55,300 ($50,401 – $105,700)	=	$12,166
24% on the next $96,075 ($105,701 – $201,775)	=	$23,058
32% on the next $54,450 ($201,776 – $256,225)	=	$17,424
35% on the next $3,775 ($256,226 – $260,000)	=	$1,321
TOTAL TAX (unadjusted)	=	$59,769

DEDUCTIBLE ITEMS

Mortgage Interest

Mortgage interest on up to $750,000 in principal is deductible. Mortgage must be for a "qualified personal residence."

Charitable Contributions

Taxpayers can deduct charitable contributions on up to 60% of adjusted gross income (AGI).

Medical Expenses

Medical expenses exceeding 7.5% of a taxpayer's adjusted gross income (AGI) are deductible.

State and Local Taxes (SALT)

Taxpayers can deduct either state and local income taxes or state and local sales taxes. Taxpayers may also be able to deduct property taxes on real estate, vehicles or other personal property. The SALT deduction is limited to a total of $40,000 per year.

Other items that may decrease your adjusted gross income (AGI):
- Traditional IRA contributions
- HSA/FSA contributions
- Dependent care payments
- Student loan interest paid
- Classroom expenses for teachers
- Self-employment expenses
- Alimony paid on a divorce or separation agreement entered into before 2019
- Moving expenses (armed forces)

For further information and updates, as well as other great resources from our Retirement Toolbox, go to https://safeguardinvestment.com/ retirement-toolbox/.

State Of Retirement

The American retirement scene is evolving rapidly.

With an aging population, the strain on government-sponsored retirement benefits seems to be intensifying. At the same time, the shift from traditional defined benefit plans (pensions) to defined contribution plans (IRAs and the like) in the workplace has placed the responsibility of investment management, market risk mitigation, and conversion of savings to retirement income squarely on individuals. This transition can present significant challenges, as many Americans grapple with understanding and effectively navigating this new landscape of personal financial responsibility in retirement planning.

By exploring various topics, such as savings adequacy, retirement age decisions, and the complexities of helping to ensure lifelong financial confidence, a 2024 study from Northwestern Mutual offers insights into some of the hurdles faced by retirees and pre-retirees.

ESTIMATING THE COST OF COMFORT:
DIVERSE RETIREMENT SAVINGS GOALS

The average amount Americans think they'll need to retire:

$1.26M

Americans believe they need $1.26 million to retire comfortably in 2025—down $200,000 from last year but similar to 2022-2023 estimates.

Retirement needs vary widely based on lifestyle and goals, leading to diverse opinions on the required savings for a comfortable retirement. Interestingly, Gen Z starts saving earlier and expects to retire by sixty-one, while baby boomers plan to work until seventy-two. Most Americans aim for retirement around sixty-five, but this eleven-year gap highlights a key principle: The earlier you start saving, the more control you have over your retirement timeline.

Source: Northwestern Mutual. "2025 Planning & Progress Study: Work & Retirement." https://filecache.mediaroom.com/mr5mr_nwmutual/179133/2025%20P%26P%20Wave%20II%20-%20Retirement%20and%20Work%20-%20FINAL.pdf. Accessed Aug. 10, 2025.

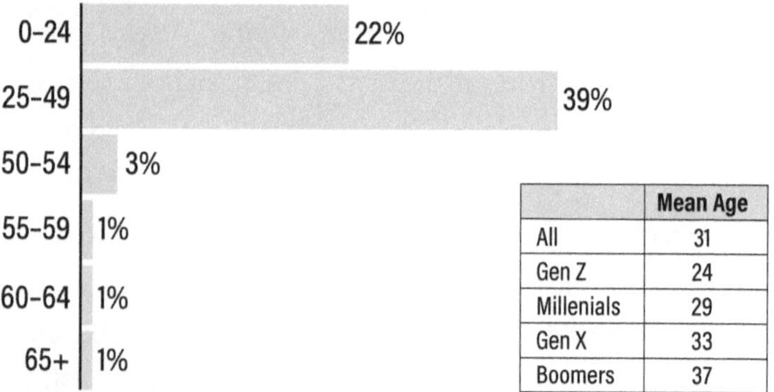

Source: Northwestern Mutual."2025 Planning & Progress Study: Work & Retirement."
https://filecache.mediaroom.com/mr5mr_nwmutual/179133/2025%20P%26P%20Wave
%20II%20-%20 Retirement%20and%20Work%20-%20FINAL.pdf. Accessed Aug. 10, 2025

Difference in the amount thought to be needed to
retire comfortably from 2024 to 2025.

-$200,000[22]

Taxes: The Often-Forgotten Factor In Retirement Planning

Only three in ten Americans have a plan to help minimize taxes on their retirement savings. Among those who do, the most commonly used strategies include the following:[23]

- Strategic withdrawals from accounts: Timing withdrawals from traditional and Roth accounts to stay within a lower tax bracket (32 percent)

- Diversifying account types: Balancing traditional and Roth retirement accounts for greater tax flexibility (30 percent)
- Charitable donations: Making strategic charitable contributions to reduce taxable income (24 percent)
- Health savings accounts (HSAs): Utilizing HSAs or other tax-advantaged healthcare accounts to cover medical expenses tax-free (23 percent)
- Permanent life insurance or annuities: Leveraging these products for their tax benefits (22 percent)
- Roth conversions: Converting traditional accounts to Roth accounts before the start of required minimum distributions (RMDs) or taking Social Security benefits (19 percent)
- Qualified charitable distributions (QCDs): Using QCDs from IRAs to satisfy RMDs while reducing taxable income (17 percent)
- Additional tax-advantaged accounts: Contributing to other tax-advantaged accounts like 529 plans (14 percent)
- Life insurance cash value: Using the basis paid into permanent life insurance cash value to stay within a lower tax bracket (13 percent)
- Qualified longevity annuity contracts (QLACs): Setting aside funds for later in retirement (13 percent)

Deciding When To Retire: Balancing Preparation With Uncertainty

Among retirees polled, it is notable that about a third had to leave the workforce for reasons beyond their control. This highlights a significant reality: Many individuals may find themselves retiring earlier than planned, often due to unforeseen circumstances.

This fact poses an important question: Is targeting a specific age or savings amount the best way to decide when to retire? Ideally, this decision should be based on a comprehensive evaluation of your financial readiness, health, and personal aspirations, rather than being dictated by external factors or default milestones.[24]

Navigating Retirement Complexity

Retirement planning is a complex and multifaceted endeavor, where understanding the difference between perception and reality can be key. It's about more than just numbers and projections; it's about crafting a future that aligns with your individual needs and aspirations.

In this journey, the true value lies in having a clear understanding of your financial landscape and how it aligns with your retirement goals.

In this context, the role of an experienced financial advisor becomes invaluable.

A financial advisor provides more than just advice; they bring clarity and strategy, helping to bridge any gap between what you perceive and what is realistic. They adeptly navigate the complexities of retirement planning, helping ensure that your strategy is not only robust and comprehensive but also flexible enough to adapt to life's unpredictable changes.

A financial advisor can be a key ally, guiding you toward a confident and fulfilling retirement, grounded in a well-informed understanding of your financial journey.

For further information and other great resources from our Retirement Toolbox, go to https://safeguardinvestment.com/ retirement-toolbox/.

Chess Terms

Activity

The first chess term we will talk about is "activity." This means the amount of freedom and space a chess piece has at any time on the board.

The rule of thumb in chess dictates that if a chess piece is stationary for too long, it loses its ability to make a difference in the game. So, keeping chess pieces in movable positions is a good sign.

Adjournment

This is an archaic chess term that is rarely in use these days. "Adjournment" means that a chess game has been stopped temporarily due to lack of time. In that case, the game gets restarted at a later time.

Nowadays, chess organizing committees make sure that all games are finished in one session. There are standard chess play rates in place these days as well. For example, almost all global chess events mandate that players should complete a minimum of forty moves within two hours.

Advantage

One of the most common terms for chess is an "advantage," which denotes a chess player's winning chances at any stage of the game. Chess commentators usually use this chess lingo when they notice that one player is in a better position than the other.

They also use similar terms, such as "slight advantage" and "clear advantage," to indicate the level of superiority of one player over the other player.

Attack

One of the most critical terms in a chess game, an "attack" is a coordinated attempt by one player to achieve an overwhelming edge over an opponent.

An attack is a great way to impose pressure on an opponent during a chess game. In most instances, attacks are planned out by a player to checkmate the rival king.

Blockade

Another technical term in chess terminology, a "blockade" occurs when a chess player stops the advance of a rival pawn by placing a piece in front. This method helps gain the upper hand during a chess game.

Backward Pawn

When a single pawn is left stranded at one place while the other pawns next to it have either moved ahead or been captured, it becomes a "backward pawn."

In this scenario, this pawn becomes easy prey for the opponent and allows the opponent to orchestrate an attack using the isolated pawn position as a strike point.

Bad Bishop

A "bad bishop" is a bishop piece whose movement has been blocked by a friendly pawn. This dramatically limits the bishop's chances of participating in the field of action, thus hindering the player's options.

Checkmate

Perhaps the most common of all terms of chess is "checkmate", which occurs when a king is placed under an attack it cannot escape. When a player's king is threatened, and no legal move exists to remove the threat, block it, or move the king to safety, the game ends immediately.

Closed

A "closed" situation arises when pawns dominate the center of the board in a way that restricts mobility. Because the central files and diagonals are blocked, pieces struggle to move freely, and both players must find creative ways to open the position.

Combination

A "combination" is a tactical sequence in which a player forces a series of moves—often involving a sacrifice—with the goal of gaining a clear advantage. These sequences rely on calculation and leave the opponent with little choice but to follow the forced line of play.

Cramped

As the name suggests, "cramped" is when a chess player's pieces are positioned too close to each other, thus significantly limiting swift movement and options of switch play.

When chess pieces are cramped, it becomes difficult for the player to make quick decisions with the pieces. Chess pieces placed too close to each other are not usually in a safe position.

Development

One of the most essential terms of chess, "development," means the slow improvement of chess pieces from their original positions to a much stronger place.

Once the chess pieces have become better positioned on the board, it is time to begin going after the rival pieces, with the ultimate objective of nailing the rival king.

Doubled Pawns

This refers to when two pawn pieces of the same color are lined up one after the other on the same column. This is typically a disadvantage because doubled pawns cannot defend each other, often becoming targets and creating long-term structural weaknesses.

Fianchetto

Derived from the Italian word fianco, meaning "flank," a "fianchetto" occurs when a player advances the pawn in front of the knight and develops the bishop behind it. This creates a strong diagonal for the bishop and is a common setup in many chess openings.

File

A "file" is a vertical column on a chessboard along which pieces move up and down. Files are labeled a through h, and controlling open files is often an important part of a player's strategy.

Fish

A "fish" is someone who fares poorly in chess matches. Hence, the term is deemed somewhat derogatory in some chess quarters.

Forced

A "forced" move is something that a chess player is supposed to go for to obliterate a lousy scenario in a game. Sometimes, a player may require more than a single forced move to save themself from an unwanted situation.

Gambit

One of the fancier terms of chess, a "gambit" is a technical move that a player engages in to gain the upper hand over the opponent. A gambit involves sacrificing one or more minor chess pieces or pawns early in the game to lead an attacking onslaught on the rival's king. Generally, gambits are used in the opening phase to bring new life to the position, create new lines of play, and generate attacking chances against the opponent.

Grandmaster

A "grandmaster" is a chess player who belongs to the higher echelons of the game's rankings. Grandmasters are brilliant chess players with very high ratings and regularly fight for the top international honors.

Horse

"Horse" is one of those terms of chess used to denote a knight, and it is an informal word primarily used by amateurs and first-timers.

Howler

A "howler" is often used instead of a chess "blunder." A howler and a blunder mean the same thing, which is a significant tactical error on the part of one chess player that proves very costly in the course of the game.

Mate

"Mate" is another word for checkmate and refers to the moment when a rival king is under an inescapable threat of capture. Once a mate is delivered, the game is over.

Material

"Material," in chess parlance, means the quality of a player's chess pieces at any given moment in a game. Someone with higher valued pieces will automatically be judged to be in a stronger position to win the game.

Middle Game

The "middle game" is the second part of any chess match. It is named as it falls between the "opening," the first part, and the "endgame," the final part.

The middle game ensues once the chess player has completed setting up and developing the pieces on the board. This is when the players begin strategizing their games to inflict damage on their opponents.

Open

In chess parlance, "open" stands for a situation in a chess match when the pieces are positioned to have enough space to move around the board, and this is the opposite of a "closed" arrangement of pieces on the board.

Opening

The "opening" is the first part of any chess game, and it involves the primary moves made by both players. During this phase, both players engage in developing their individual pieces while also securing their positions.

This is a time when players move their kings to a safe and secure square/tile, having good defensive cover. Players employ a variety of opening moves to experiment with their play.

Over The Board

In the digital age, and especially after the pandemic, more and more chess players are switching to online chess portals to compete against each other. Under these circumstances, some chess terms are becoming more popular.

One among those is the expression "over the board." This means that two players are playing a match on an actual chessboard while being physically present on the spot.

Passed Pawn

When it comes to terms of chess, "passed pawn" is an expression used to denote a pawn that has escaped enemy pieces on the board and is safely on its way to the farthest square of the board to get promoted.

From the player's perspective, this is a very favorable position, as the passed pawn most likely reaches the other side of the board to be promoted to a higher-valued piece.

Promotion

Intricately linked to the previous term, passed pawn, "promotion" in chess means a situation when a pawn crosses all barriers on the board to reach the last square of the board to be promoted.

When a pawn gets promoted, the player handling the same can opt for any of the higher valued chess pieces, be it a queen, a bishop, a knight, or a rook.

Queening A Pawn

The expression "queening a pawn" denotes when a pawn gets promoted to a queen. This is a highly advantageous situation in a match, giving players an extra powerful piece at their disposal.

Rank

A "rank" refers to a set of horizontal squares or tiles on a chessboard from left to right or vice versa. To give you an example, at the start of any match, all the pawns are stationed next to each other on the second rank of each side.

Rating

A chess "rating" is a numerical measure of a player's overall playing strength. The world's chief international chess governing body, the Fédération Internationale des Échecs (FIDE), adheres to the Elo chess rating method to rank players worldwide.

Sacrifice

"Sacrifice" is one of those terms of chess that we frequently hear during chess commentary, and it refers to the intentional loss of one or more chess pieces to gain an advantage during a game.

Sealed Move

A rare instance these days, a "sealed move" is a secret move that is not played but recorded in an adjourned match. When the game resumes at a later date, the recorded action is played, and the battle continues.

Space

As can be understood from the word itself, "space" refers to a condition in a chess match when ample room exists for both players to maneuver their pieces on the board.

Smothered Mate

A type of checkmate, a "smothered mate," takes place when an enemy king is barred from making an escape when faced with a mate by its own pieces.

Stalemate

A stalemate occurs when the player whose turn it is has no legal moves available and is not currently in check. When this happens, the game ends in a draw.

Study

In chess, a "study" refers to a composed endgame puzzle created to illustrate a particular idea or theme. These positions are crafted to highlight beautiful or instructive solutions rather than occurring naturally in live games.

Sudden Death

When two chess players have a fixed amount of official time remaining to finish a game, it is referred to as the "sudden death" period.

Tactics

Integral to the essence of a chess match, "tactics" refers to those sets of moves that players employ to initiate threats and counterthreats at one another.

Tempo

"Tempo" is an Italian word that translates to time. In chess, though, this term is not used to designate the time each player has on the clock. Instead, it is a way to identify each turn a player spends to move a piece. When we want to refer to more than one tempo, we use the term tempi.

APPENDIX E

Works Cited
And Author's Notes

1   Edward R. Brace, *An Illustrated Dictionary of Chess* (Chartwell, 1981).

2   Patrick Kiernan, "Which Is Greater? The Number of Atoms in the Universe or the Number of Chess Moves?," National Museums Liverpool, accessed December 3, 2025, https://www.liverpoolmuseums. org.uk/stories/which-greater-number-of-atoms-universe-or-number-of-chess-moves.

3   Mark Kolakowski, "The 5 Most Important Lessons From the 1929 Crash That Matter Today," *Investopedia*, November 1, 2019, https:// www.investopedia.com/the-5-most-important-lessons-from-the-1929-crash-that-matter-today-4774814.

4   Kate Ashford and Roberta Pescow, "What Is IRMAA, and What Are the 2024–2025 IRMAA Brackets?," NerdWallet, October 14, 2022, https:// www.nerdwallet.com/article/insurance/medicare/what-is-the-medicare-irmaa#.

5   Jackie Stewart, "Roth IRA Basics: 11 Things You Must Know," Kiplinger, November 5, 2024, https://www.kiplinger.com/retirement/ retirement-plans/roth-iras/602323/roth-ira-basics-10-things-you-must-know.

6   "Social Security History," Social Security Administration, accessed November 18, 2025. https://www.ssa.gov/history/imf.html.

7   There are many actuarial lifespan calculators available online.

8   Go to ssa.gov for the most current eligibility information.

9   Emily Guy Birken, "Your 'Longevity Literacy' Can Make or Break Your Retirement Planning," Fast Company, September 30, 2023, https://www.fastcompany.com/90959041/good-retirement-planning-requires-longevity-literacy.

10   Caroline Smith, "Are Older Adults Financially Prepared for Long-Term Care?," The Long-Term Care Poll, accessed January 14, 2025. https://www.longtermcarepoll.org/are-older-adults-financially-prepared-for-long-term-care/.

11   Jamie Hopkins, "Long-Term Care Planning Misconceptions Are Holding Back Advisors and Consumers," Forbes, updated April 11, 2018, https://www.forbes.com/sites/jamiehopkins/2018/04/11/long-term-care-planning-misconceptions-are-holding-back-advisors-and-consumers/#7f0338af3bf9.

12   Christy Bieber, "What Is Probate & How Does It Work?" Forbes, June 15, 2023, https://www.forbes.com/advisor/legal/estate-law/what-is-probate/.

13   Julia Kagan, "Irrevocable Trust," Investopedia, September 9, 2022, https://www.investopedia.com/terms/i/irrevocabletrust.asp.

14   Kagan, "Irrevocable Trust."

15   Kagan, "Irrevocable Trust."

16   Safeguard Investment Advisory Group, LLC, "Protect Yourself Against Identity Theft," October 2024, accessed December 3, 2025, https://safeguardinvestment.com/wp-content/uploads/2024/10/FINAL_Identity-Theft-Protection-Sheet.pdf.

17   "Gen X Nearing Retirement with Worries About Limited Savings, Allianz Life Study Finds," Allianz Life, September 25, 2025, https://www.allianzlife.com/about/newsroom/2025-Press-Releases/Gen-X-Nearing-Retirement-With-Worries.

18   Daniel de Visé, "For Gen X Retirement Bites," USA Today, September 27, 2025, https://www.usatoday.com/story/money/2025/09/27/gen-x-retirement-bites-savings-inflation/86365380007/.

19   de Visé, "Gen X."

20   de Visé, "Gen X."

21 de Visé, "Gen X."

22 "A Better Way to Money," Northwest Mutual 2024 Report, accessed December 15, 2025, https://www.northwesternmutual.com/2024-annual-report/.

23 "Planning & Asset Allocation Mix Progress Study 2024, Work, Retirement, & Taxes," Northwestern Mutual, accessed Nov. 6, 2024, https://news.northwesternmutual.com/planning-and-progress-study-2024.

24 "ALI Cannex Protected Retirement Income and Planning (PRIP) Consumer Report," Alliance for Lifetime Income, May 17, 2024, https://www.protectedincome.org/wp-content/uploads/2022/08/2024-PRIP-Chapter-1-Release-May-17-2024.pdf.

www.ingramcontent.com/pod-product-compliance
Lightning Source LLC
Chambersburg PA
CBHW022101050726
47591CB00002B/621